THE KILRO

Zakiyyah Alexander, Christina Anderson,
Jaclyn Backhaus, Tanya Barfield, Clare Barron,
Kate Bender, Hilary Bettis, Jocelyn Bioh, Rachel Bonds,
Jami Brandli, Bekah Brunstetter, Sarah Burgess,
Sheila Callaghan, Eugenie Chan, Sam Chanse,
Mia Chung, Eliza Clark, Alexandra Collier,
Fernanda Coppel, Erin Courtney,
Frances Ya-Chu Cowhig, Sarah DeLappe,
Lydia R. Diamond, Jackie Sibblies Drury, Laura Eason,
Larissa FastHorse, Halley Feiffer, Lindsey Ferrentino,
Leigh Fondakowski, Madeleine George, Sarah Gubbins,
Dipika Guha, Karen Hartman, Amina Henry,
Laura Jacqmin, Hansol Jung, MJ Kaufman,
Nambi E. Kelley, Georgette Kelly, Boo Killebrew,
Basil Kreimendahl, Kimber Lee, Martyna Majok,
Mona Mansour, Meg Miroshnik, Rehana Lew Mirza,
Anna Moench, Dominique Morisseau,
Julie Marie Myatt, Janine Nabers, Mary Kathryn Nagle,
Lynn Nottage, Jiehae Park, Lisa Ramirez,
Theresa Rebeck, Gabrielle Reisman, Amelia Roper,
Melissa Ross, Sharyn Rothstein, Tanya Saracho,
Laura Schellhardt, Heidi Schreck, Jenny Schwartz,
Jen Silverman, Charise Castro Smith, Ruby Rae Spiegel,
Susan Soon He Stanton, Kate Tarker, Stephanie Timm,
Mfoniso Udofia, Paula Vogel, Kathryn Walat,
Timberlake Wertenbaker, Calamity West,
Leah Nanako Winkler, Bess Wohl, Lauren Yee,
Stefanie Zadravec, and Anna Ziegler.

THE KILROYS LIST

THE KILROYS LIST

97 MONOLOGUES AND SCENES
BY FEMALE AND TRANS PLAYWRIGHTS

VOLUME ONE

Edited by Annah Feinberg for The Kilroys

FOREWORD BY PAULA VOGEL

THEATRE COMMUNICATIONS GROUP   NEW YORK   2017

The Kilroys List is published by Theatre Communications Group, Inc., 520 Eighth Avenue, 24th Floor, New York, NY 10018-4156

The publication of *The Kilroys List*, through TCG's Book Program, is made possible in part by the New York State Council on the Arts with the support of Governor Andrew Cuomo and the New York State Legislature.

TCG books are exclusively distributed to the book trade by Consortium Book Sales and Distribution.

ISBN 978-1-55936-535-2 (paperback) / ISBN 978-1-55936-856-8 (ebook)

A catalog record for this book is available from the Library of Congress.

Book design and composition by Lisa Govan
Cover art by Alex Reeves

First Edition, June 2017
Third Printing, January 2023

CONTENTS

FOREWORD

By Paula Vogel

S ometimes the best allies playwrights can have are critics.
To prove this point, I'd like to bring up the *Washington Post*'s Peter Marks, whose initiative led to "The Summit," a community discussion hosted by Arena Stage, with a panel comprised of artistic directors of Washington, DC, theaters.

I wasn't there. But thanks to Twitter, I was a fly on the wall. Peter Marks asked the artistic directors why there were so few women playwrights produced in DC. One of them responded: "Because they are not in the pipeline."

According to my Twitter responses, there was consternation, indignation, and just plain anger in the audience.

As I read my Twitter account, I must confess my response: resignation.

When I first became a playwright in 1974, women comprised sixteen percent of all playwrights produced in America. In 2014, we increased up to seventeen percent. And, after forty years of speaking out at conferences, summits, festivals, and panels (and getting a reputation as an "angry dyke"), I turned my advocacy to running playwriting programs. For forty years

I searched for feminist writers, writers who stretched the theatrical and gender envelope, playwrights who would create fully dimensional, complicated character recipes for women. Playwrights who would create female Willy Lomans and Hamlets, or bring to the stage complex Linda Lomans and Ophelias, which their creators had never envisioned.

One writer at a time, I hoped to mentor more daring, more collaborative, more inventive, and more confident writers who had chutzpah to self-produce. Every year during admissions, I sifted through piles of plays on my living room floor. It was sheer anguish to narrow down the playwrights whom I was dying to work with—from two hundred to forty . . . and then finally to three. My living room floor was overflowing with plays that deserved cornucopias of pipelines.

Alas, my own program at Brown (and Brown raised complete funding—and shouldn't all art programs be free?) reproduced an economy of scarcity that mirrors the economy of scarcity of the major institutional theaters. I realized there was no way I could provide such a cornucopia, running a program single-handedly. Neither could my colleagues in the field who also put their own writing on the back burners to mentor: Naomi Iizuka, Marsha Norman, Tina Howe, Connie Congdon, Rob Handel, Steven Dietz, Sarah Ruhl, Laura Schellhardt, Christina Anderson, Quiara Hudes, Julie Jensen, Christopher Durang, Oliver Mayer, Velina Hasu Houston, David Henry Hwang, Lynn Nottage, Erik Ehn, Kathleen Tolan, Chuck Mee, Mac Wellman, and Deborah Stein, just to name a few. (Remember the old adage: "Those who can, do; those who can't, teach"? That's another myth worth discarding, alongside the one about "the lack of women and writers of color to put in the pipeline . . .")

Dear readers: Let me tell you, however delayed the gratification might be, during the past few years my hope has become renewed as I witness the generations of writers who are more inventive, more daring, and more collaborative than ever. We owe thanks to 13P, a revolutionary group of playwrights (talk about feminist!), who collaboratively produced each other, one play a year, and then shuttered their not-for-profit doors after the thirteenth production. They gave us a role model to follow: Do not wait for permission from the institutional theaters to be produced.

And thanks to the Guerilla Girls, whose subversive tactics have been calling attention—attention must be paid to them!—I fondly remember reading their stickers in the bathroom stalls of institutional theaters: "In this theater, the taking of photography and the production of plays by women are strictly forbidden."

And then there were the Lillies: Julie Jordan, Marsha Norman, and Theresa Rebeck, and countless others who were determined to celebrate women in theater, fundraising to provide fellowships, space, and time, through new initiatives. (If you happen to be in New York during one of their cabarets or award celebrations, please go! Their generosity and joy is infectious. Women and men gather together to put the spotlight on women's achievements that often go unheralded by the Tony Awards or the press.)

And at last there are the Kilroys. A group dedicated as women and transgender artists to say: "We were there. We are here." A group dedicated to the proposition that there is an abundance of prodigious talent and creativity that must replace the current pitiful trickle through institutional pipelines. A group of kick-ass theater artists who declare there is no excuse, in the twenty-first century, for producers and artistic directors to insist they cannot find women or women of color in the field. The incredible Kilroys List makes visible proof that there are infinite playworlds of which our current pipelines can only dream.

The Kilroys reward and thank the theater companies that don't offer excuses, but *do* their work, produce the most exciting work by women playwrights side-by-side *with* the exciting work of our male colleagues. They present each producing theater with a Cake Drop, an event in which they bake a cake for a producing theater. (How subversive to show that women playwrights, who belong in a key creative role, writing at their computers, can whip up a mean cake in the kitchen, too!)

Oh and may I talk about feminism? I realize the definition of that word morphs as much as sexuality and gender do with each generation. But I do want to take a moment to advocate for the embracing of this word. There is no feminism without the inclusion of and accessibility to all races, all classes, all sexualities, religions, and ethnicities in our country. When I was sixteen, my brother gave me a copy of *Sexual Politics*, and he told me: "You have a mind: Use it."

To me, feminism always embraced men as well as women. To embrace feminism is to insist that all of us are able to embrace a spectrum of gender and sexuality in our theaters, film, our parenting, our bedrooms, our lives. And that spectrum must be represented on our stages. Men who are playwrights should know that they are being produced in theaters that do select the best, most daring, and deepest plays—and not just the status quo of the Boys' Club.

It does a disservice to us all. We have minds. Our theater companies can no longer be wasteful in their programming, skipping over the exhilarating voices of this volume. The Kilroys have amassed writers aplenty to fill hundreds of pipelines.

Um, may I jettison the pipeline metaphor? Pipelines flow from one source, instead of many; pipelines funnel the resources (water, sewage, fossil fuels) in one direction to one destination. I would rather have rivers, tributaries, creeks, than a pipeline.

Where once I had my nose pressed to the window glass outside the candy store, this book opens the door to us all. Welcome. Greedily, I have read each monologue, and now I'm hungry to see each play onstage.

Thanks to all the Kilroys. Your daring and generosity make us all dare; I find myself, after reading this book, not as resigned as I was when I started. Thanks for the hope. Back to the computer.

Providence, Rhode Island
May 2017

PAULA VOGEL is the Pulitzer Prize–winning author of *How I Learned to Drive*. Her other plays include *Indecent, Don Juan Comes Home from Iraq, A Civil War Christmas, The Long Christmas Ride Home, The Baltimore Waltz*, among others. She has also had a distinguished career as a teacher and mentor to younger playwrights, first at Brown University and currently at the Yale School of Drama.

ABOUT THE KILROYS

The Kilroys: "We make trouble. And plays."

The Kilroys are a gang of playwrights and producers who came together in Los Angeles in 2013 to stop talking about gender parity in theater and start taking action. We are named after the iconic graffiti tag "Kilroy Was Here," which was first left by WWII soldiers in unexpected places, a playfully subversive way of making their presence known.

We set out to mobilize others in our field and leverage our own power to support one another. In 2014, we released our first annual "List" as a response to systemic gender bias in theater programming. It compiled the top unproduced and underproduced (one professional production only) plays written by female and trans writers, nominated by hundreds of professional artistic directors, literary managers, professors, producers, directors, and dramaturgs, all who had seen or read a minimum of forty plays the previous year.

Each respondent recommended three to five plays each. The List comprises the most recommended plays from this survey. To ensure unbiased results, responses were anonymous. All identifying information of recommenders was tracked separately from their recommendations via the survey software. The members of The Kilroys did not nominate plays for The List.

The vetted collection of industry-recommended works was designed to bring worthy plays by female and trans playwrights to the forefront of the American Theater conversation. It is a tool for producers committed to ending the systemic underrepresentation of female and trans playwrights in the American theater.

This first printed collection includes a monologue or scene from each play from the 2014 and 2015 editions of The List. It represents an abundance of excellent new work by female and trans playwrights, and reflects a wide ethnic, geographic, and aesthetic diversity.

The founding members of The Kilroys are Zakiyyah Alexander, Bekah Brunstetter, Sheila Callaghan, Carla Ching, Annah Feinberg, Sarah Gubbins, Laura Jacqmin, Joy Meads, Kelly Miller, Meg Miroshnik, Daria Polatin, Tanya Saracho, and Marisa Wegrzyn.

For more information about The Kilroys, visit: www.thekilroys.org.

With special thanks to Rachel Viola.

The Kilroys
May 2017

THE KILROYS LIST

ZAKIYYAH ALEXANDER

Girl Shakes Loose Her Skin

An overqualified black girl finds herself in New York City, single and unemployed. Now, she's got to figure out where home is. A three-city journey about growing up when you're already grown. In this monologue, Ella (thirties) confronts her ex who shows up unannounced at her house in Oakland, California. This is especially tense because her ex broke up with her and essentially disappeared. It's the third-act showdown that's been building for the whole play.

ELLA: Just like you to show up unannounced.

Not. A. Word. Didn't even answer my emails. I mean what the fuck? You evaporated from my life. That's some psychotic shit. Made me feel like I meant nothing to you, and all I did, *all* I did, was open up my life to you. I fed you. Made plans with you. Do you realize how fucked up that is? Do you understand what you did to me?

Were you held hostage by the enemy? That's the only acceptable excuse. I have serious trust issues, and you knew all my insecurities and you're all, "I'm being honest." Fuck you. You don't care about anybody but yourself; you're selfish. Should know better, but no, I'm the one thinking we're falling in love—I was wearing good underwear and you had your bags packed. I mean, who does that? Do you realize all you had to do was break up with me if you wanted me out your life? But you had to be such a—just looking at you is getting me so. I mean, why? You make me so, so—gah!

CHRISTINA ANDERSON

The Ashes Under Gait City

Simone The Believer, an online guru, attempts to break away from the internet and build a community in Gait City, Oregon. During Emancipation, the city pushed out its black residents, and Simone wants to take back the city. In this linear narrative, Simone (along with her assistant named D, who is also one of Simone's first clients) slowly acquires a series of local black residents (including property owner Felicia), who fall under her leadership. In this monologue, Simone posts a YouTube video, calling for members to join her in Gait City:

SIMONE:
My people! My people!
Good morning, good evening, good night, good times.
I send you love and blessings.
This is yours truly: Simone The Believer in you/in me/ in us/in we/as one.
I know it's been a minute since I uploaded a video.
I've seen the posts on my wall, my timeline, all up in my email . . .

Ya'll tryin' to know where I'm at!
And everyone will know soon enough.

(As the video continues, the following encounter takes place onstage:
Felicia introduces Clay to Simone.
Clay is visibly nervous, excited, and in awe.
Simone is gracious, warm, attempts to ease his anxiety.
Clay may shed a tear or two.)

But first . . . I want to talk about somebody I recently
    met.
I just met a brother named Clay.
He's been watching my videos, been down with my
    teachings for years.
Almost since the beginning.
And earlier today, for the first time, he and I stood on
    common ground,
Greeted each other face-to-face, eye-to-eye. And it was
    glorious.

Clay recently packed up his life, and moved to Gait
    City, Oregon.
And he told me fate guided his journey.

(Simone hugs Clay. She walks beside him as they exit.
Felicia follows.
The video continues:)

Now, you know how Paris is The City of Lights?
Well, I think of Gait City as The City of Disregard.
Almost two hundred years ago, the residents of this
    city made a decision that affects this area to this
    day.
Almost two hundred years ago, the black population
    in this city was erased.
Google it. It's crazy.

So fast-forward. Today in this moment and you will
    find my new friend Clay.
A brother who decided to claim a space in this City of
    Disregard.
After a lifetime of being pushed out of neighborhoods
    he once considered a haven,
Clay decided to pick up his life and settle in Gait
    City, Oregon.

Fate guided my journey as well.

Like Clay, I have settled in Gait City. And I will invite
    a chosen few to join me.

Together we will create a community of like-minded
    folks
To honor the ancestors erased from this city and
    revitalize the legacy
That exists today.

Let me ask you:
Have you claimed your space?
=.=
=.=
Are you sure it's yours?
=.=
=.=
Clay grew up feeling displaced.
Do you hold a similar feeling in your spirit?
=.=
=.=
I have a community. You could be the perfect fit.

Make a video. Sixty seconds.
Tell me who you are,
Who you want to be,
And what skills you bring to the table.

There will be a forty-eight-hour submission window.
Be honest, determined, and clear.
Ya'll cain't half-ass it in my house, okay?

I'll contact the chosen ones directly.

Be love. Be light. Be-lieve. I'm out.

Man in Love

*This play is written in heightened language and told through multiple
scenes. The pace is swift with moments of drama and humor. Set
during the Great Depression, characters try to survive in a fictive
segregated city. A young black serial killer, Paul Pare, Jr., goes about
unnoticed as he claims victim after victim. In this monologue, Paul
Pare, Jr. walks in the black neighborhood, aka "The Zoo," and hunts
for his next victim. (Text surrounded by two asterisks "**" denotes
dialogue with characters unseen by the audience.)*

PAUL PARE, JR.:

    ** Good evening. I'm sorry, sir. No, I don't have any
       change to spare. **

    Five is a prime number. Meaning it can only be
       divided by one and by five.
    Meaning five is divisible by itself. Five is divisible by
       one.
    It is divisible by one.
    She, the prime number, is divisible by me—the one.
    Number Five walks these streets of The Zoo, waiting
       for me to smile at her.
    I smiled at the First One,
    Offered to buy a drink to Number Two,
    Helped the Third One with her bags,
    Spotted the Fourth One while buying a jar of peach jam.
    And now I wait for Number Five to walk towards me.

** Good evening, miss. **

(The woman walks past Paul Pare, Jr., ignoring him.)

That was not she. She will not be Number Five.

She will be a Negro woman with a young face.
Big brown eyes full of questions. Her curiosity will
   out-muscle her fear.
Like this one here . . .

** Hello, miss. Good evening. **

She is divisible by me.

** Do you mind if I walk with you for a bit? **

My ease slips comfortably into hers.

** I'm enjoying this cool weather. How about you? **

It is divisible by one. By some one. One is me. She is
   divisible.

** You coming from work? **

The human body consists of 206 bones . . .
Gray bones. Pink flesh. Beautiful brown skin.

** Me? I work at the library . . . restocking books,
   repairing broken spines, torn pages . . . **

It'll be so nice to have some body *new* at home
   waiting for me.
   That really is something nice.

** I really like that scarf you're wearing. Blue is a very
   pretty color on you.

Brings out your eyes. **

I walk with her. She walks with me.
She is Five. Divisible by me.

JACLYN BACKHAUS

Men on Boats

Men on Boats *charts John Wesley Powell's 1869 expedition, sanctioned by the U.S. Government, to chart the Colorado River and its canyons. An ensemble cast of ten rides a raging river in its quest to map the last blank space on the American map.*

The characters in Men on Boats *were historically cisgender white males. These roles should be cast entirely by people who are not. I'm talking about racially diverse actors who are female-identifying, trans-identifying, gender-fluid, and/or nongender-conforming.*

In this monologue, John Wesley Powell, the one-armed leader of the expedition, puts Dunn, a fellow crew member, in his place after a disastrous run on the river causes Dunn to loudly question Powell's leadership skills.

POWELL: Well. Some of you are here for sport and some of you are here for skill and some of you are here because you get a kick out of killing bears and some of you are here because it got your ass out of the army on a good note and some of you are here because you have nowhere else to go. You know why I'm here? I'm here because my friend, the fucking PRESIDENT of the UNITED STATES, needed a better knowledge of the arid lands of this nation. I am here because I was given a job. And in case you didn't know, it's hard for gimps to get jobs around these parts, so I am going to do this job to the best of my ability. And it just so happens that I've run more rivers than any of you all put together—I did the fuckin' Mississippi up and down when I was seventeen years old and I've done more tributaries than you can name on BOTH of your sorry hands. If you want to go over what we could have done to save the No-Name, then be my guest. But, instead of that, I am going to focus on the marvelous forethought we put into divvying up most of our supplies between each boat. And I'm going to thank God that none of us perished today, and that none of us broke any crucial bones. All of that is a win, in my book. We won't make it to the end of this expedition if we focus on anything other than wins. So, if you don't want to go down to the wreckage tomorrow, then I'm sure I can rely on one of your fellow crew members to be a good sport.

You got your fucking cliff, Dunn. Now how about a nice fucking rabbit dinner.

(Hawkins, the cook, plates up a fine plate and gives it to Powell. Powell passes it to Dunn).

Who's next?

TANYA BARFIELD

Bright Half Life

Erica and Vicky's relationship spans a lifetime of love, marriage, parenthood, and heartache. As the play shuttles back and forth in time, we see various moments from their lives. This speech refers to an event early on in their relationship (before the play begins) in which Vicky broke up with Erica. At the time, Vicky told Erica that she loved her and Erica offhandedly responded that "love fades." This speech occurs at the end of the play, flashing back to this pivotal moment decades earlier, as Erica reimagines or relives that moment. (Note: Erica has an intense fear of heights.)

ERICA:

> I don't want it to fade
> So I don't want to overuse the words
> Because some day maybe we'll want to have kids
> I mean I want to
> and I think you do too
> We're dating—were dating (past tense)
> but you can just tell that we might be one of those
>   couples

major not minor
And don't you think, don't you think
that we're gonna (we might, I think we might) watch
    our kids get married
we might make chicken soup for each other in the rain
don't you think we're major not minor
when you smell the coffee brewing in the morning
you'll think of me because I'll be the one making the
    coffee
and when you close your eyes at night
you'll think of me
because I'll be the tiptoes that you don't hear
    tiptoeing to bed
and I'll be the one whose lips will bring you kisses
and the smell of oranges in January
I don't want it to fade
I'd give you more than a life if I could
and I'm not s'pose to say that because how long, how
    long have we been dating
not that long
even though I just know
You might say, you're young (we're both young) and
    you don't know what's a lifetime
But I'd give you days
and nights
the sun, moon, and clouds if I could
on a string
you could fly them like a kite
they'd fly you
That's what's in those three words you say I was
    afraid to say
That's what I wanted to say
Take me.
You want to go hang-gliding or skydiving or
    parasailing or wherever
Take me
to all those places you want to go.

The Call

Peter and Annie (a white couple) are hosting a dinner in celebration of their decision to adopt a baby from Africa. Drea (Rebecca's newish girlfriend) has been probing Peter for a story about a trip to Africa that he went on decades ago with his best friend (and Rebecca's brother) David. David's life ended tragically and neither Peter nor Rebecca ever talk about him. But, tonight is a happy occasion and Drea blindly asks questions, demanding that Peter talk. Acquiescing, Peter begins the following story lightheartedly, almost comically. Peter is unprepared for where the memory finally takes him.

PETER: . . . One time, I remember, out of nowhere, we got invited to this family's house for dinner. David made friends with everyone—and somehow through hand signals, we get invited. But then, we don't go. We're both sick, heatstroke, and we're chugging Pepto-Bismol, so we don't go. A couple of days later, we go. The directions are: "Such and such village. The house near Kafele's house," but nobody knows who Kafele is! We wander around calling out, "Kafele? Kafele?" Seems like Kafele isn't actually important; he's just some guy. Eventually, we get there, apologize for not coming when we were supposed to; the wife's crying. Her eyes are puffy and the husband looks like he's been crying, too. And their daughter is so frail, she looks like she hasn't eaten in weeks. It turns out— now these people are very poor, they have nothing, their farm is barren—it turns out they slaughtered their last goat for our dinner. And we didn't show up. It was. Awful. But they forgive us; they're so nice we feel like they're our long-lost family but nobody really says anything because we don't speak the same language; we just use hand signals. We stay until it's late, then we leave their straw hut, go back to our hotel room, slip into our cozy beds and go to sleep. After a month—no, actually more—we're still talking about it, so we decide to buy them a goat. We try to push the goat up the hill but we fail. Goats are very stubborn. So we hire a goat herder.

We finally get there, they are so appreciative, they start to cry. *(Beat, remembering)* And . . . their daughter is missing, and . . . we ask where she is. She died. *(Beat. Trying to uplift the mood)* Well. That wasn't a very uplifting . . .

CLARE BARRON

Dirty Crusty

You're never too old to learn ballet. Or at least that's what Jeanine hopes when she starts taking adult ballet classes from an ex-ballerina named Synda who's opened a dance studio in her small town. What starts as an unconventional student-teacher relationship quickly turns into an infatuation and intense friendship. Up until this point in the play, Jeanine has been our protagonist and, in addition to her closeness to Synda, she has been involved in a very new and very sexual relationship with Victor. Out of necessity, Victor ends up taking over Jeanine's role in the ballet recital. Here he talks with Synda about the first time he ever saw a dead body. They're taking a break from dance practice—sitting on the floor, drinking beers.

VICTOR: So when my granddad died my grandma was all pissed at us because nobody wanted to go down there and see his body because my mom hates dead bodies and my mom's brother hates dead bodies. So my brother and I were like, "We'll do it." But we didn't tell anyone ahead of time because we were afraid we would chicken-out.

And we get down there and the dude at the desk is super friendly and creepy. Like, "Right this way. You can find Mr. McCreary in Room 107," like we were there for some business meeting or something. And we stand in the hallway. Just in front of the doorjamb. And I start freaking-out because I know if I go one step closer, I'm going to see my granddad's dead body. And I say to my brother, "I don't know if I can go in there." And I start crying because I've always been a crier. And my little brother is kind of holding my arm. And we're standing in the doorway—huddled together—like these two scared little deer. Just shaking. And we start shuffling towards the doorway. Just shuffling. Inch-by-inch. We do not cross the threshold. We do not step into the room. My brother's keeping it together better than I am. We're only eighteen months apart. And then we see him. And it's a relief. Because it doesn't look like him at all. And I start laughing and I realize that we're still technically in the hallway and the creepy, friendly dude is watching us but I can't step into the room. I can't do it. And I say to my brother, "He doesn't look like him at all." And my brother says, "Look at his hands." And I can't tell if he's saying that because his hands look like the hands of a corpse, or because his hands look alive and that's how he recognizes him . . .

And we probably only stand there for three minutes, or something. Not very long. And I'm so proud of myself for doing it and not chickening-out. But now I wish I would've gone up and stared straight in his face, you know. Taken a good look. He was such a weird color of pink. Anyway. We drive back in my brother's silver jeep. And inside it's all warm and cozy and my little cousins are trying to get us to go down to the motel with them so they can swim in the pool. And my brother and I go to find our grandmother and she's in the closet look-ing through her shoes. Trying to pick out a pair for the funeral tomorrow. And we tell her what we did and she just says, "Bless your hearts. Bless your hearts." And then she calls out to our mom, "Cindy? Do you know what these boys did? They went down and saw Granddad. Did you know about that?" And my mom says that she didn't know. And my grandmother turns back to us, still clutching her loafers, and says, "Well bless your hearts."

You Got Older

Mae, thirty-two, is back in Minneapolis after a rough several months. She lost her job, got dumped by her long-term partner, and wound up back home in a small town in the Pacific Northwest to help take care of her dad who has a rare, aggressive form of cancer. She's been stressed-out and heartbroken for so long that happiness sneaks up on her.

MAE:

And I'm out walking
Further than I've walked in months
And the whole world is cold and white
But the cold feels kind of good on my face
And I feel warm in my coat
And I keep walking
All the way from my apartment to downtown
        Minneapolis
Until my feet get cold and wet with sweat
And I duck into a Trailblazer looking for some boots
All the snow boots in all the world are sold out online
I'm not joking. This is not a joke
They are actually sold out
Because people are freaking-out
About the Polar Vortex
So I'm not particularly hopeful when I duck into this
        Trailblazer
But there's a man there holding a box of insoles and
        he says they have one pair left. Sorels.
"What size are you?"
"I'm a size seven."

"Shoot. These are sixes."
But I try them on anyway
And they fit!
"Sorels run big," I tell him. (His name is Eric.)
"They're not making any more this season," Eric says.
"That's crazy! They're all sold out!"
"You better be careful walking home. People are
    going to try to steal those boots from you."
And Eric calls me "the luckiest girl in all of Minne-
    apolis." And I walk home hugging those boots
to my chest.
And in the elevator of my building
An old lady is talking to the doorman
He shouts at her, "Pea Soup is better! I want Pea Soup!"
"Sure thing, Bob. I've just gotta get some—"
Elevator closes.
"Hambone."
She turns to me, explaining, "I've known Bob for
    twenty-five years. We make things for each other.
    It's cool"
It is cool
"That's what friends are for!"
And I go into my apartment
And I put on my boots
And I think about what I want to eat for dinner
And I start to feel something
That I haven't felt in a while
In a long while
What is this feeling?
Happiness
For no reason at all
Just happiness
Just standing in my living room wearing boots
Just full
Of happiness
For no reason
Just standing in my boots
All alone.

KATIE BENDER

Still Now

After witnessing the fall of the Twin Towers, Annie heads to Japan to study Butoh, looking for a dance form that expresses the destruction she can't comprehend. Ten years later, Annie is diagnosed with stage-four cancer and returns to Butoh to prepare for her final dance. At the neighborhood clinic for the first time, Annie finally admits to the doctor that she suspects something is really wrong.

ANNIE: No no wait. Remember that tornado last week?

    I was on Myrtle, late for a student, I can't sleep anymore, all day I'm exhausted, I had a fever, I was rushing down the street and that wind just blows me into this bodega—

    Listen.

    The point is I could smell everything! The cat piss and the bleach and the cigarettes. This fridge was getting blown down the street, like floating down the street, with the door banging open and it was filled with rotten bananas and meat and I could smell it all.

    I can't eat. I can't sleep, I can't work.

Something is really wrong with me.

I've known my body my whole life. This is something different.

HILARY BETTIS

The Ghosts of Lote Bravo

This play is a fierce and uncompromising drama set in the modern-day slums of Ciudad Juárez. It follows the journey of Juanda Cantu, a maquiladora worker, as she hunts for her missing teenage daughter. This is a world where violence, uncertainty, hunger, and survival are the circumstances these people live in every moment of their lives. There is no room for reflection, political commentary, emotional indulgence, or judgment.

The trap of this world is playing the language as lyrical or as a telenovela. It is not. It is raw and street. These people are unapologetic fighters, even into death. Juanda (who is very Catholic) has begun praying to La Santa Muerte for visions of her daughter's life. This is the first time Juanda has brought an offering to La Santa Muerte— a bottle of cheap tequila bought with hush money from a police officer.

LA SANTA MUERTE: Hand me the bottle of cheap tequila.

(Juanda reluctantly does. La Santa Muerte takes a sip.)

Coca plants harvested in rural Columbia by a poor farmer who was shot by a rival's son for his crop. I knew this farmer. *He prayed to me.* Heated on a stove and turned to paste by the rival son. He was stabbed to death by two brothers who robbed him for six hundred pesos. I knew this rival son. *He prayed to me.* Two brothers drove the paste in their truck through Panama, Costa Rica, and Nicaragua to a lab in Honduras. They were shot by a woman working for the lab. I knew these brothers. *They prayed to me.* The woman mixed the paste with acid and turned it into cocaine. She was drowned by her boyfriend when she asked for a break after thirty-six hours of breathing fumes. I knew this woman. *She prayed to me.* The boyfriend drove the cocaine in his boat from Honduras to Mexico. He sold it to three boys who poisoned him. I knew this boyfriend. *He prayed to me.* Three boys carried the cocaine through Mexico to the American border where they bribed a police officer to turn a blind eye. He took their money, then turned another blind eye when an American border patrol agent drown them in Rio Bravo and took their cocaine. I knew these boys. *They prayed to me.* This bottle of tequila purchased with the money from that police officer. I know this man. *He prays to me.*

(La Santa Muerte finishes the bottle.)

You bring me blood money when I asked you for a fucking sacrifice.

The History of American Pornography

This play is a dark family drama that walks a fine line between fantasy and reality, with a lot of comedic elements (I hesitate to call it a "dramedy" since I think that sets the wrong tone). It follows the journey of Star Papazian, who grew up in the family porn business, and is now looking back on her life in search of intimacy and human connection. The time spans from 1974 to 2014 in San Fernando Valley, California.

This is one of Star's memories. New Year's Eve Y2K. Star and Jackson Marsh (twenty-seven, male, handsome, and charismatic) met at a party at the Playboy Mansion, and have come back to Star's place. After several moments of drunkenly making-out, Jackson pins Star to the ground and pulls out a video camera, revealing his true intentions.

JACKSON MARSH: I had an older sister named Marissa, and she didn't get along too well with my step-dad. So she took off to L.A. when she was sixteen. Got a job as a waitress. She seemed happier than she'd ever been living at home. She said she believed, for the first time in her life, that she had a future. Then a month went by . . . Two months and I hadn't heard shit from her. One day I get a package from her. A note that says, "I'm sorry. I was desperate for money and couldn't ever come back home. I love you, Jackson. Always remember that." And a tape, a porn tape of her and two guys, a Dolls-and-Stripes Production being filmed by a guy named Old Man Artie.

(He begins to cry.)

She killed herself. My sister . . . I would have given her the money. I was only thirteen, but I would have . . . I would have sold my fucking kidney! I miss her so much . . . The thought of, of men out there jerking-off to my dead sister . . . That, that's all the world will remember her by . . . *A whore.*

JOCELYN BIOH

Nollywood Dreams

Nollywood Dreams *is a comedy set in early 1990s Nigeria at the rise of the Nigerian film industry. Gbenga Ezie, one of hottest directors in Nollywood, has written a new script that every actress in Nigeria is clamoring to be in—and hopefully play the lead role of Comfort. When Gbenga's old flame, Fayola, returns to Nigeria, she quickly becomes a front-runner for the role. In this scene, Fayola confronts Gbenga and makes him face the truth of her feelings toward him from both the past and the present.*

Note: this play is set in Nigeria and all characters are to be played by black and/or African actors. West African/Nigerian accent required.

FAYOLA:

So, you think a "fresh start" is sitting in a
cold apartment, in a scary city, miles
away from my family, waiting for you
to come home at night? Lying to
everyone that you were doing so well
at NYU film school when you were just a

janitor? Or are you talking about the
"fresh start" you were trying to have
with that white girl? And
how did that plan work out for you?
Hmm? That white girl dropped you
faster than you could turn your head . . .
Just like every other African man—
you were sick with "American Fever."
Don't you understand, to them, you are
nothing but another black man? A nigga
with an accent . . . *(Beat)*
You think I didn't
hear about how she turned you over to
immigration? Hmmm? And how they sent you back
    on a plane
home without anything . . . Barefoot . . .
Like the stupid African you are. And look at you now.
    Still *only* concerned
about yourself. Only concerned about
what people are saying about you, you,
you! *(Beat)*
Before I left Nigeria, I had it all: a
wonderful career, fame, money, family,
and good friends. I was happy. I didn't
need American success—I had my own—
right here. And I left it all behind
because I believed in you and your
dreams . . . But you never thought about
me . . . You never cared about me or
what I was going through. Just took off to Los Angeles
    with that
white girl trying "sell your script."
. . . And you didn't call, come back, or
apologize to me. Not even once . . . Not
even now . . .
And after all these years, here I am,
trying to piece together my career
again. Asking you of all people, to give

me back the chance to reclaim all I
have lost trying to help you succeed . . .
Do you know what this is like for me? You always
    said you wanted to "make
me the star." Here is your chance.

RACHEL BONDS

Swimmers

This play is a comedy with a strong undercurrent of tragedy—or perhaps the other way around. It begins in the basement of an office building, and moves up every floor, scene by scene, until it ends on the roof. Some characters reappear, some do not. It is a strange day at the office on this Monday—there have been coyote sightings in the industrial park, and eerie billboards spotted on the way to work touting the upcoming end of the world. Everyone is struggling to get through the day. Randy (Sales, 2nd Floor) had his own unsettling experience over the weekend, something he just can't shake, and details the events in this speech to his co-workers, Priya and Tom.

RANDY: Oh! So— Wait—guys—I wanted to tell you—I had the most intense thing happen this weekend.

Okay, so I was out—I went for this run on the green-way—and, yeah, God, it was *so intense.*

Okay, so I was running, right? And I got to the end of the greenway, where that picnic area is? And I actually found this . . . little path, I guess it was, that went into the woods. So I ended up following it, actually . . . for like, a while . . .

And I'm going along and going along, and the woods are getting dense at this point, like the path is getting narrower and kind of hard to follow, I'm not sure if I'm even on any path anymore, and then I see there's this little . . . I wouldn't call it a house, exactly. More like a hut.

So—I get closer and I see it's like a real person's home. Like there's pieces of clothing hanging around, and weird little, like, glass ornaments and chimes and things made of twigs and bird feathers and stuff. So I'm thinking I should turn around at this point, you know, since I'm worried I'm trespassing on some crazy medicine woman's property or something, and I'm so far in the thick of it now that if I screamed, I doubt anyone could hear me. So I'm turning around and looking for the path and she comes out. The woman who lives in the hut.

So, I'm thinking, Oh my God. She's going to eat my kidneys with a machete or something is what I'm thinking. So she steps out of the hut, clearly because she's seen me from the window, and I kind of wave and say, Oh sorry, I'm just lost, sorry. And she gestures for me to come back toward her and I say, No that's okay I should be getting back. And then she says, If you're going to be peering in my windows then I'd at least like to know your name.

So I say, Oh my God, sorry, it's Randy. And she says, Hello Randy. And she has this. This voice. It's like the most . . . I don't know how to even describe . . . like the most soothing—it's like when I was a kid and I'd wake up in the middle of the night and through the wall I could hear my parents talking to each other in the other room. It had that low quality—like, well—I'm not explaining it well . . . but you know what I mean. So she says, How are you, Randy? And I say, Oh, you know, I'm fine. And she says, Let me look at you. And I say, What? And she says, Let me. Look at you.

So then I step closer and she looks at me, and I look at her, and she has these eyes, like, this color that's aquamarine or or or turquoise—like a color that no one's eyes could possibly be unless they're wearing tinted contacts, but this is this woodland creature of a woman, in a hut, in the depths of the woods, and there's no way she's wearing tinted contacts. And so I'm like floating around in this, like, amazing sea of her eyes and she's staring at me and she says, Randy. The time has come.

And she touches me, here, with the palm of her hand.

And then she just goes back inside.

And shuts the door.

And I . . . turn around.

And eventually find the path I was on and head back to the picnic area.

The Wolfe Twins

This play takes place in a modest but very clean B&B in the Trastevere neighborhood in Rome. Lewis, newly forty, invites his estranged sister Dana, thirty-nine, on a trip through Italy to reconnect. Old wounds soon fester, particularly when Lewis befriends the other guest staying in the B&B, Raina, a visual artist from Boston whose husband mysteriously continues to not show up. Raina gives this speech near the end of a very drunken, wild night with Dana and Lewis.

RAINA: You guys . . . I'm going to admit something to you.

I didn't leave my room at all today. I mean, until we went out—I was just in my room, just sitting there. I was just in there, like, doing absolutely nothing.

No, but— It's an ancient city, I'm supposed to be out wandering around and taking in all the, you know, taking it all in and seeing shapes and lights and color that I don't get to see in stupid—Boston—and I just didn't do it, I just was in my room, just—

(She shakes her head and laughs) And this was supposed to be the big apology trip!

Because . . .

I let this—man—feel me up in the hallway at this—at my friend's art opening. Eh, no, that makes it sound like he cornered me and was like, ooh, hey let me touch you or—whatever—but that's not what it was—I was just there in the hallway with him and it was such a lovely night, it was a beautiful show and I was so taken with it, there were all these—because my friend has been working on this series of exploding houses—they're these wonderful, kind of haunting paintings of houses, like, flying through the air, and just beginning to—like you can just see the beams just starting to split apart, but he's caught them all at the moment just before everything goes flying away from each other . . . they're so, just . . . I don't know, I love them, you know?

. . . So I was there, sort of just floating along through the evening and then I let this guy put his hand up my dress.

(She laughs.)

It was so weird! Like we weren't even ourselves, we were just these little clay figures—like little sculptures of real people I saw from above, like moving around in this funny puppet way . . .

I don't know, I guess I thought it could be this kind of small, secret thing that I could just—have—just to myself—something to . . . help me feel like I'm not suffocating at every moment of every day, but . . . I, uh . . . yeah, that didn't work.

(She sips her wine and laughs.)

(Singing out) Maaaarriaaaage!

JAMI BRANDLI

Bliss (or Emily Post Is Dead!)

1960. North Orange, New Jersey. Clytemnestra and Medea are now housewives with a pill addiction, and Antigone is a teenage girl in love with a black boy. On the surface, they're all seemingly blissful to follow the etiquette "rules" of Emily Post. Then Cassandra, a black working girl, moves into their neighborhood and all routines are interrupted. Cassandra is determined to finally break the curse of Apollo, the egotistical god who gave her this "gift" of prophecy but made it so no one would ever believe her. His curse is practically indestructible: all she has to do is convince someone to believe her. Can Cassandra convince these women they now have choices in this modern era? Can all four women escape their ongoing fate?

Maddy (Medea) has just learned that her husband, Jason, is leaving her and her sons, Bobby and Timmy, for his boss's daughter. She's enraged, but she decides to take a more interesting approach in her revenge. Maddy addresses Jason and her two sons as she frenetically bakes scones for Jason's new wife-to-be.

MADDY: Toasted crumpets, toasted crumpets . . . *(Growing dark)* *. . . toasted crumpets, toasted crumpets, TOASTED CRUMPETS.*

(Maddy clasps her hands. She then removes her robe to reveal a pretty dress. She draws a smile on her face and goes to the table. At the table, she transforms into the blissful housewife as she makes toasted crumpets in a large mixing bowl.)

Honey. Darling. Sugar pie. Dearest. Jason.

(Maddy speaks and mixes the batter with vigor and spunk.)

I was thinking about what you said about moving up in the world and that the only way to do it is by marrying your boss's daughter. Well, I've come to the conclusion that you are right. You should positively go for it! It's become clear that I won't help you get anywhere in this new decade of the 1960s. But I do appreciate you plucking me from Honolulu and planting me here in North Orange, New Jersey, where you promised to grow me the real American Dream with two kids, a house, a car, pleasant neighbors who would accept me as long as I'm exactly like them (HA!), efficient home appliances like this handheld mixer here, and your eternal love. I believed you because my love was—IS—my love IS so so so so so powerful. But alas, I hold no prestige. No key to your future. No wind for your sails. I am holding you back, my sweet. But how kind you are to allow me to continue living here, in our house, with our sons. You really didn't have to do that, but I—we—appreciate it. But that's the kind of man you are, Jason. Thoughtful.

Bobby and Timmy, isn't your daddy just so thought-ful? Of course they think that!

(Maddy laughs, stops, then resumes mixing vigorously.)

I want to show you that I have absolutely, positively, one hundred percent NO bad feelings toward you and your boss's daughter. SO, as a token of my wishing you two love birds well, I am making her a batch of my toasted English crumpets with this handheld mixer you so thoughtfully purchased for me. I'm going to finally get these toasted crumpets right this time! You can count on me.

(Maddy winks. From under the table, Maddy pulls out a large dark bottle. She uncaps it and pours the black liquid into the bowl.)

What's in this bottle, you ask? This is a special flavoring from the Hawaiian Islands. I snuck it into my bag the day you and I left Honolulu after the war ended. I figured I'd take it just in case of an emergency. Because you never know, right? Anyway, it's an extract from of one of Hawaii's native flowers, Angel's Trumpet. Doesn't that just sound divine?

(Maddy winks. As she takes out handfuls of the batter and slaps them onto the baking sheet, HARD!)

But don't you worry. It won't be too exotic. The Angel's Trumpet adds a hint of a magical kind of sweetness. And you know just how sweet I can be, Jason.

(Maddy winks. With a big smile, she holds up the tray.)

There. All I need to do is bake these and let them cool and then I will give them to your boss's daughter myself. Oh, I think that would be best, don't you, Jason? That I present them to her to show that I give your new relationship my blessing? Of course you do.

(She laughs, then stops.)

Now Bobby and Timmy, do not, do not, do not, do not, DO NOT TOUCH THESE CRUMPETS! You listen to Mommy like you always do, okay? Okay. This is for

Daddy's new wife for his new life and we want to give her every single crumpet we've got.

(Maddy winks again, smiling hard.)

BEKAH BRUNSTETTER

The Oregon Trail

The Oregon Trail *follows Now Jane, an angsty middle-schooler in the 1990s, obsessed with the Oregon Trail computer game, through her disappointing adult life; and Then Jane, a girl traveling the actual Oregon Trail with her family. In this scene, overworked and underpaid Mary Anne has had it with her little sister Then Jane, who has a sadness she cannot shake. She has been holed up in her house for months, drowning in white wine and Easy Mac and decidedly not looking for jobs. She can no longer take it.*

> *(Violently, Mary Anne throws a dish onto the floor. She stops. She breathes.)*

MARY ANNE: You wanna know what's wrong with you? You are selfish and you are lazy and you smell like PARME-SAN CHEESE. I work hard all day, I come home, I want *home*, I want QUIET, and there you are, sitting there all day, doing nothing. YOU ARE NOT CUTE. You suck. You make me sick. Mom and Dad let you get away with this shit, but not me, I RUN A NINE-MINUTE MILE. And you sit around with my futon up your ass, watching my TV, that I NEVER get to watch, I pay for it! I GET UP AT FIVE A.M., and you are PATHETIC. I AM VERY TIRED.

(She stops, breathes hard. Both are stunned.)

You have not experienced tragedy.

The woman who brought her dead two year old into the ER last night after she accidentally ran over him with her secondhand minivan right after her husband was killed overseas, SHE gets to not get out of bed. Not you.

Mom and Dad won't say this to you, but I will. I can't live with you anymore like this. And I know you don't have anywhere else to go. But I mean it, if you don't at least TRY to change your—perspective, your—whatever it is, then you are out, because I love you, but you look stupid when you're sad and you have no good reason to be.

So I need you to figure out what's wrong and I need you to fix it.

And I love you but you look stupid when you're sad. So I need you to figure out what's wrong and fix it. FIX IT.

SARAH BURGESS

Camdenside

This is a comedy about a great white shark named Doug. After his wife is killed in a boating accident, Doug drives around Florida in a motorized wheelchair on a furious hunt for revenge. He is accompanied by a small fish named Terry who sprays him with salt water at regular intervals. When Doug and Terry take shelter in the basement of an apartment building, Doug disrupts the lives of the humans who reside upstairs, and his loneliness becomes more than he can bear.

Doug goes through his notes from the previous night's detective work. Note: Terry is too small to be heard by the audience. Ellipses ". . ." indicate when Terry is speaking.

DOUG: Terry.

Terry.

Are you listening?

. . .

Let's organize our notes from last night.

. . .

You can say it was disappointing, but I don't see it that way. I say, okay good, we've searched half the road, and since we didn't find it, we've gotta be close. I know we're close. I have a great sense for looming success.

. . .

All right. Please take this down. I don't want to double-back next time we search.

Let me know if you remember any of this differently.

. . .

(Reading his notes with one of his eyes) The first building was a two-story pink house with two automobiles in the driveway. No boat.

The second was a blue house with two young people out front. One auto. No boat.

The third was that large gray building, right?

. . .

Okay yes no you're right. The third was that small yellow house with a collection of decorative lawn statues in the front yard. That's right. No boat.

The fourth building was an orange house, two stories. No boat.

And then there was a large gray building with no windows. Near the top a lit sign said "A T ampersand T." No boat.

After that there was that very large parking lot. Because our vehicle tops out at eight miles per hour, it took us approximately two hours to search that parking lot. No boat.

. . .

What?

Okay, 2.5 hours spent searching the parking lot.

. . .

No I'm sure you're right.

. . .

Yeah I agree, we should note time spent. It'll help us plan going forward.

After the parking lot was the light brown apartment building. Two bicycles and three automobiles. No boat.

The seventh building was a store. The sign said "Raheem's Vacuums." Did I explain to you what I think a vacuum is?

. . .

I did, Okay.

The eighth building was a store with food and drinks. Many autos came and went. Five adolescents engaged in pre-mating rituals in the parking lot. One seemed left out. The sign above the entrance said "seven one one."

No boat. Is that about what you remember?

. . .

Great.

And then there was a beige apartment building. No boat.

. . .

At that point, my hunger became overwhelming and you pointed out a seagull sitting on a mailbox. Oh shoot.

SHEILA CALLAGHAN

Women Laughing Alone with Salad

This play is a feminist fantasia riffing on the popular internet meme of the same name. This monologue takes place at the top of the play where Guy (late twenties, male) is speaking to his mother on the phone.

GUY: . . . Okay maybe you're on a work call or getting a facial or whatever, maybe that's why you keep sending me to voice mail . . . or, maybe you just don't wanna talk to me 'cause you'd rather send commands from on high and expect me to comply without further question . . . and I told myself I wasn't gonna leave a message 'cause you never listen to them anyway . . . but here I am. So.

    I got your text. And here's my answer. No. I'm not buying your fucking priest boyfriend his top-shelf booze again. You can buy it yourself. I'm tired of it. I'm not your employee. I'm the wet fleshy blob you expelled from your vagina twenty-nine years ago, and I don't appreciate being manipulated. I have a life. A job. I mean both kind of suck right now, but they're still mine.

Also dinner this week sounds great. Looking forward to it.

Also. I can't hang up. Because I know that the second I do, I'm gonna walk to the liquor store, plop down my credit card, and buy your priest boyfriend his top-shelf booze. Because I'm dead inside.

(Beat. He hangs up. Exits.)

EUGENIE CHAN

Madame Ho

Madame Ho *is inspired by the life of my great-grandmother who ran a brothel in Barbary Coast, Chinatown. The play tells the story about Ho, a madam who tries to raise her daughter Daisy right, amidst the struggles of the brothel and its women. Daughter Daisy's hormones are exploding, as she lies awake at night listening to the sounds of beds squeaking, men and women crying and sighing and making other unexpected sounds of joy and sorrow.*

Here is a couple she overhears: a laborer, tired after a long day's work, admires the bound feet of Rose, his favorite woman. Both the laborer and Rose are completely dressed.

LABORER:
　　　　Like little pieces of jade.
　　　　Precious precious.
　　　　Curve of your foot
　　　　Very pretty.
　　　　So many crinkles and folds.
　　　　You smell like fermented rice.

The rice I slurped the day my son was born
He must be three now

Or seven
Or eight
Or could he be thirteen.
He must be tilling the fields;
Perhaps he is riding the water buffalo.
Naughty boy.
I must have the scholar write a letter.
Send it back home
Scold him.
I must tell his mother:
Keep a careful eye on him
Make sure he keeps the pig well.
He must not slack.
He must be a good son.
He must be.
His mother will see to that.
His mother . . .

(He sighs.)

His mother's feet are cracked, dry.
I will send her extra money for ointment
His mother's left foot is ridged with scars running
    north to south.
She stepped on a scythe.
I had to carry her on my back.
We plastered the wound with fresh mud and herbs.
Clumsy woman!
I did not even know she had hurt herself,
She kept threshing.
"The harvest is in," she cried, "such joy!"
Sometimes her feet are bitten by leeches.
She lets me pull them off
My how thick and hard her feet are.

(He is quiet.)

> My, how happy I am to be here in *Mei Gok* [America]!
> Happy without her disgusting feet.
> Happy to rest my tired head
> On your lovely golden lilies.
> I am indeed a lucky man!

(He rests his head on her feet and weeps. She strokes his hair, silent.)

SAM CHANSE

Fruiting Bodies

The play takes place in a fog-enveloped forest just north of the Golden Gate Bridge. It is a comedy and tragedy involving limited visibility, the interfamilial politics of race and gender, thought experiments pushed to extremes, and no wifi.

When Ben gets lost on a routine mushroom-hunting expedition, his semi-estranged adult daughters, Vicky and Mush, reluctantly head into the woods to retrieve him, only to wind up losing their bearings. This speech takes place shortly after the sisters arrive in the forest. Mush has wandered off and lost sight of Vicky.

MUSH:

> Hello, tree. You are beautiful. You are a beautiful tree.
> Hey, come over here, there's a beautiful tree!
> Okay, I know you can hear me.
> Look, you're annoyed by the whole me-getting-fired
>   thing, I get it.
> I was inspired by idiots.
> I read about this Russian guy who defaced a Rothko
>   at the Tate. He just walked up to a fucking Rothko

and wrote directly on it with a marker. Just like
   that, in a world-famous cultural institution,
   writing on a painting worth several million dollars.
The words he wrote were:
"A potential piece of Yellowism."
The meaning of which may not be immediately
   apparent;
it's about this organization or movement he was part
   of—Yellowism.

Which wasn't really an organization or movement:
Yellowism is not art, and Yellowism is not anti-art.
   And it is not *not* art.
Basically it defies category.
They have a whole manifesto and website and
   YouTube videos explaining in really circuitous
   language what "Yellowism" is:
It's an element of contemporary visual culture.
It's not an artistic movement.
It's not art,
it's not reality,
it's just
Yellowism.
The way it works is, you put something in a "yellow
   chamber"—and you can declare anything a
   "yellow chamber" by being one of these two guys,
   and signing your name on it—and then whatever
   is in the yellow chamber becomes a work of
   Yellowism and loses everything it was before. It's
   freed of its former meaning.
All the possible interpretations are reduced to one—
are equalized,
flattened to Yellow.
A Rothko isn't a Rothko anymore, it's just Yellow.
   Flattened.
They stop being works of art,
and they become pieces of Yellowism.
Art already exists.

Yellowism is a new context.

So people wanted to know, "*Why* would you do this?"

And after spewing out a lot of incoherent bullshit, the guy says,

"It is very difficult in the contemporary art world to say something,

to make people listen.

It is very difficult to do anything in this world anymore that anyone will notice."

Right? It's like a howl for recognition.

The cry of anguish of today's post-post-social media-ed, networked world.

It's so hard to *be* anything,

but at the same time there's so much pressure *to be some*thing.

So it's dumb what they did. I'm not saying it's cool.

But the heart of it? The pain driving it?

They just, didn't want to let a Rothko be a Rothko.

So if you put aside the whole muddled description and self-justification aspect of it, there's actually the seed of a worthwhile thought experiment there.

Hello, tree. You are a beautiful tree.

MIA CHUNG

You for Me for You

As they attempt to flee the Best Nation in the World, North Korean sisters Minhee and Junhee are torn apart at the border. Each must race across time and space to be together again: Junhee navigates the surreal Land of the Free in order to return safely to rescue Minhee. In the meantime, Minhee—a loyal North Korean citizen—has fallen down a well at the border, and there ensues a venture through the treacherous terrain of personal belief. In this monologue, Minhee has come to the end of her journey in the well.

MINHEE:
  Junhee was right.

(Minhee covers her face. With a deeply felt groan:)

  Little sisters are never supposed to be right.

(Minhee is very weak. She stands up, loses her balance, slides back to the ground.)

I must grow wings and fly out of here.
I will be a worm and dig myself out.
I can find a door in solid rock and open it.
But . . . I'm tired. So tired.
And I need something to eat.
Because I'm hungry now. So hungry.

I'm hungry to hear Beethoven and see a windmill and
    learn Spanish.
I want to drive a car. I want to know what air-
    conditioning feels like.
I want to see the blue sky.

I want to put it all in my mouth, spit the seeds out,
    and chew.

(Minhee looks upward, then shouts to the top of the well:)

I'm hungry now! I'm so hungry! Junhee, I'm hungry,
    do you hear me?
Can anyone hear me?

ELIZA CLARK

Future Thinking

This play takes place at Comic Con where Peter, an obsessed fan and pet photographer, is being held in violation of his restraining order by Jim, a security officer who dreams of being a cop. Elsewhere in the hotel, Chiara (the object of Peter's obsession) is tormented by her stage mother and her bodyguard, who are secretly sleeping together. This monologue takes place at the end of an hours' long interrogation of Peter by Jim. Peter has just accused Jim of being a "very sad human being" who messes with people because he can. This speech is Jim's response.

JIM: You're saying I'm like Biff. Like Biff from *Back to the Future*.
    I got a sick kid you know. Not the fat one. The other one. My daughter. She's just a baby, two years old. She's got bone cancer. I don't expect you to say anything. I'm just telling you, things aren't always what you think they are. You might want to chew on that for a second.
    Doctors say she's dying.
    It's a shame. You know, obviously for us it's the tragedy of our lives, but for the world, you know? Because

this kid's got something going on, something real special. 'Course I think that, right? She's my kid, but objectively, I'm saying she's got something special. Like, and this is just a little thing, but for months, we've been putting our trash out on the street for the truck and we come out in the morning and the cans are all fucked-up, trash everywhere. I thought it was kids. Teenagers, or kids at my son's school fucking with him, teasing him for being a fatty. But then, last week, Stella, that's my daughter, she's doing this thing that she does sometimes, playing lighthouse. She sits on her bed and she points a flashlight out the window, flashes it around, like a lighthouse. Stupid. Anyways, she's flashing the light around and she points it at this tree, and there's four sets of eyes all lit up at the top of this really tall tree. Raccoons. That's who's been fucking-up our trash cans. And I'm all pissed-off, getting ready to take a chainsaw, cut the tree down, bash these fuckers' heads in with a baseball bat. You know, really take out some rage on these poor fucks. And Stella's like, "No Daddy." And then she points the flashlight up at the tree and she says, that one's the daddy, that one's the mommy, that one's the Ruben, that one's the Stella. They're a family, you know? Two years old, but she can see that.

Goddamn raccoons are gonna live longer than my kid.

ALEXANDRA COLLIER

Holy Day

Cal and Tim are traveling the world on an unconventional honeymoon to third world countries and exotic locales. When Cal discovers a photo of a woman she's never met in Tim's passport, she leaves him to spend a day wandering the city alone. In this monologue, she is sitting by the window of their hotel, looking out at the boy she spent the day with, telling Tim about her day. Cal also does the gravelly voice of the god statue she bought—almost ventriloquist like. The god's voice is demarcated to make the switch clear.

CAL: Well he thinks he's a man but really he's a boy. He must be all of eighteen. At first he wanted pens so I gave him all my pens. And then he started following me everywhere. He makes these chirping noises like a little bird? With his hand outstretched. I was weaving through this market and he just kept hanging on, following me around, chirping, and I couldn't breathe and he was pulling at my skirt and I couldn't breathe, and he became like this black speck in the corner of my vision so finally, I stopped him and I said: "You can walk with me but we walk as friends."

For some reason that stopped him chirping. So we walked and he led me places. He tells me stories. I'm not always sure what he's saying. But they seem to be funny stories and when he grins, it's lopsided—he smiles sideways, his jaw is wonky and for some reason that makes everything seem completely hilarious.

We had lunch together. The way he ate. I've never seen someone *so* happy to see food. I was there picking at the noodles—no appetite—and he was cramming it all into his mouth. And when he finished, I pushed my plate over to him and he thought this was so shocking and hilarious and stupid and he covered his mouth and laughed. And I said, "Go on." And he giggled and giggled and giggled . . . *(Deadpan)* and then he devoured the whole thing.

And then we walked around and everyone else seemed to be having a siesta or something because the streets were empty and he kept pointing at things, explaining who the different gods were—painted in orange and gold and blue above the door frames. He would point at one, and I would say, "What's that one do?" And he'd answer, "Strong" or "Warrior" or "Jealous." One-word answers but his English was good. And then we got to this incredible building, crumbling with these twisted columns and a tiny blue god smudged on its side and he pointed at it and said, "Lies." At first I didn't understand what he meant but then I worked it out. It's the god of truth. It can see through lies. So I bought one at this antique shop next door.

(Cal pulls an ugly blue god statue out of her backpack.)

I've been talking to the god since I got home. Asking it questions. The weird thing is, it just keeps giving me the same answers.

(She picks up the god-like puppet. Cal does the deep and strange gravelly voice of the god throughout. Her responses are quick, right off the back of her questions.)

Does he love me?

GOD: Lies.

CAL: Does he love her?

GOD: Lies.

CAL: Will he be faithful to me?

GOD: Lies.

CAL: Does he touch her the same way he touches me?

GOD: Lies.

CAL: Will we make it?

GOD: Lies.

CAL: It's reassuring in a way. That everything is a lie. Don't you think?

FERNANDA COPPEL

King Liz

Liz Rico (forties/fifties, black or Latina), a successful sports agent, is attempting to convince Freddie Luna, a potential client, to sign with her. Liz is certain that Freddie could be a star basketball player, a high earner. Liz is at the top of her game here; she knows how to pander to her (potential) clients' egos and when to remind them that she's the only one who can take them where they want to go. She is also asking Freddie for something in return—it's all part of the game.

LIZ: Let me tell you a little something about who I am. My mom died of cancer when I was three because my father couldn't afford her treatment, so when I got a full scholarship to Yale, my goal was to grow up to be someone who could pay to kill cancer.

Now I've got a penthouse on the Upper West Side overlooking Central Park. My neighbors are Steven Spielberg and Oprah Winfrey, and I got a house in the Hamptons next door to Commissioner Adam Silver. Within the last three years, my current client roster has collectively made over nine hundred million dollars. I am the only woman to have been on the *Forbes* "Most Powerful Sports Agent" list three times and on *TIME Magazine*'s "Most Influential" list twice. Nobody can stop me. No one. Not even God.

What I can offer you as an agent isn't anything you can buy. It's my marrow, it's the tenacity that led me to this table. I will fight for you to be successful the way I fought for myself to make it in this world that doesn't want people like us to succeed. I make that promise to you in exchange for a commitment. I need you to promise that you will stay out of trouble.

ERIN COURTNEY

Honey Drop

Diane, a famous but mentally unstable poet, drives cross country in an RV with a young admirer, Xander, in order to reconnect with her son, Max. In this monologue, Diane has taken mushrooms and is tripping in a pet cemetery. Diane believes she is talking to Max, but he is not there.

DIANE:

I am so glad you are doing well, Max.

(Diane starts to sob a bit.)

Why can't it be simple?
I love you
And just simple like that.
What's wrong with us that we make it so hard?
Me. What's wrong with ME that I make it so hard.
You're healthy, Max, and strong.
You must have got that from your dad.
'Cause my side is all messed-up.

You know that I have tried every type of medication
    there is.
They work for a little bit and then they stop working.
And sometimes writing worked
And the attention helped
But I always needed more of everything
I always had to up the dose
And then change the medication—
And I wasn't there for you
And that's the devil in it.
That's the devil
Of the thing.
And I'm sorry, Max.
I'm sorry that I wasn't there for you.

Oh. There's a deer over there. And it's looking right
    at us.

Can we be saved, Max?
Can we?

I Will Be Gone

I Will Be Gone *is a play about grief and regret. After her mother
dies, eighteen-year-old Pen goes to live with her aunt Josephine in a
small town in the California High Sierra Mountains. Pen gets a job
as a tour guide at the nearby abandoned, gold-mining town. This
monologue takes place at the ghost town, Bodie. It is a very windy
day, bright sun, and Pen is very hungover.*

PEN *(Reading from clipboard)*: Welcome to Bodie, the largest
    ghost town in the country!
        Bodie was one of the richest, and most violent, gold-
    mining towns in all of the West.
        There were a dozen industrialized mining companies,
    saloons, brothels, and gambling halls. One girl, when

she learned that her family was going to move to Bodie, famously wrote in her diary, "Good-bye God, I am going to Bodie!"

Bodie was first discovered by a prospector named Wakeman S. Body. He found gold, staked his claim, but that very first winter he got lost and died from hypothermia. They did not find his corpse until the snow melted in the spring. In Wakeman Body's honor, they decided to name the new town after him. Although a sign painter made a mistake and the sign painter wrote B-O-D-I-E instead of B-O-D-Y. The town liked the new name and so they kept it.

As quickly as the town grew, it fell into a rapid decline—the mines dried up, the economy of the town went bust and this thriving, Western boomtown was soon abandoned. Lucky for us, the state of California acquired the land, declared it a national historic park *and* mandated that Bodie must be kept in a "state of arrested decay." That means that it is against the law to repair or alter any of these buildings. So, if a building is in danger of collapsing, they can prop it up with a support beam but that is the only addition that is allowed. "Arrested decay." I think that is a pretty poetic term.

On our tour, you will be able to peek into the windows of the saloon, the schoolhouse, the church, homes, and the general store. Like looking into the past, you will see relics—pencils, spectacles, canned goods, beer bottles, pots and pans—that have been untouched for a hundred years.

The mines were very dangerous places to work.

Miners died from flooding, explosions, fire, and suffocation.

The miners told stories about spirits in the mines.

The miners heard otherworldly, menacing knocks in the mines.

(Pen begins knocking on her clipboard, ominously.)

And so they named these spirits Tommyknockers.

Miners reported that they would hear knocks just before a mining tunnel would collapse.

Some miners felt the Tommyknockers were benevolent spirits. Dead miners sending a warning out to the living. "Get out. Get out. Get out. Before it is too late."

But other miners felt the Tommyknockers were evil spirits. Angry spirits that wanted to exact revenge by causing the tunnels to collapse. They believed the Tommyknockers were there to *take* lives not save them.

(Pen stops knocking.)

Once the mines all closed down, families in nearby towns began to report knocking sounds in their homes. The patient, repetitive knocking was said to foretell danger and death.

FRANCES YA-CHU COWHIG

The World of Extreme Happiness

Sunny is a nineteen-year-old Chinese peasant turned-factory girl. She's been working as a janitor at Jade River Manufacturing in Shenzhen for the past four years. She has been selected by the factory management to be the "model peasant" introducing a propagandistic pseudo-documentary "Factory Girl," a PR event designed to rehabilitate the public image of the factory after a string of worker suicides. During her speech, Sunny goes off-script and decides to use the opportunity to advocate for real change.

> *(The Great Hall of the People. Beijing, China. 2012.*
>   *Sunny takes the podium. Dozens of camera flashes illuminate her face.)*

SUNNY *(Into microphone)*: Ladies and gentlemen, esteemed foreigners, press, and business people, good morning. My name is Sunny Li, and I am here to tell you how leaving the countryside to work in a city factory gave me the opportunity to transform my life, support my father and the education of my little brother, Pete.

Life in the countryside was lonely and hard. Factory life is exciting and full of new challenges. I have hundreds of friends. We go everywhere together. Thanks to me, my brother graduated high school. My father treats me like a son, and is so proud I'm supporting our family. I'm so grateful to Jade River Manufacturing for improving the lives of so many peasants, including me, and my best friend. Ming-Ming.

(Sunny looks up. Short pause.)

When I first got to the factory I didn't like—I hated who I was. I thought the problem was me. So I went to night school and studied self-improvement. I put marbles in my mouth. Bleach on my skin. Every month I tried a new hair color. One day I was walking past a building covered in shiny windows, and saw the reflection of a city girl in it. It was me! Then two people from Beijing asked me for directions. It felt like the beginning of success—even city people thought I was one of them! I didn't know it wouldn't matter how much I looked like a city person—or how many people I tricked, because my ID card said peasant.

City people. They think they can burn through peasants. Like a . . . a natural resource. To them we're coal. We don't have the same rights, but . . . we're supposed to make them rich.

I want to say, to my fellow migrant workers—I am sorry for trying to be different. I thought . . . I thought it was the only way I could—save myself. And change my destiny. But destiny—it's not something one person can change. We have to work together and make—demand— change. For all of us.

(A police officer enters and turns off Sunny's microphone.)

My section manager jumped out a factory window. There was a . . . petition by his body. Filled with hundreds of signatures. Every name was a protest. I protest—and I ask you to protest with me. Demand you get the same rights as people born in the city. Go on strike. Stop working. And if they still say no—go home.

Let city people try to live for a single day without us. Stop selling them food and sewing their clothes. Let the city people go hungry. Let them walk naked on the street. Without shoes. And live in houses with broken windows and—

(Lights shift. The crowd and press are gone. Sunny is alone onstage. Inward, to herself:)

Chop off my arms—I can still strike! Hack off my legs—I can still walk! Rip out my heart—I will mysteriously recover! I can bathe in boiling oil and come out cleaner than I went in!

(A police officer places a black hood over Sunny's head.)

SARAH DELAPPE

The Wolves

Over five scenes, we've seen an indoor girls soccer team warm up for five consecutive games. Now one of them has died, #14, Megan. This is the team's first game after her death, and they're all gathered on the field. Soccer Mom is Megan's mother. She meant to bring orange slices. Frank is their old coach, the father of the team captain, #25. #2 has an eating disorder; earlier we saw her binge on orange slices. Alex, or #7, was Megan's best friend. This is the first time any teammate is referred to by name, as opposed to by number.

Soccer Mom walks onto the field. She is really the nicest mom but manic with grief.

SOCCER MOM:
  hi!
  hi gals!

  (a small collective hi)

  wow
  you look so

wow!
my god!
it's you guys!
it's our gals!
you're not getting any younger
you know?
you all look so
and it's just
it is so good to see you
just
just
just
like so good

(a pause
    she lets out a sharp laugh)

I said
ha
listen to me
ha
"like"
ha
"like" "like" "like"
in our house we have a quarter jar
Alex I know you've seen it
a quarter for every "like"
and for "um" every "um"
and the oh the what do you
the going up? at the end? of the sentence?
what is that
and the *(imitates)* baby talk the little
but
they hate it
the girls
they just hate it
and I've tried to explain
if you're saying something is "like" something

then it isn't the same
it's just "like" it
and if you say that
and you hem and you haw and you um and you make
    everything?
a question?
then no matter how you know awesome
how brilliant your thought is
no one will ever take you seriously
because you sound like an idiot
and one time I said
I was mad
I was really
she didn't do the dishes or was texting at dinner or uh
(trying to remember) I don't uh
I don't

funny

(she is lost in thought then sudden and snapping)

"MEGAN you say "LIKE" because you don't know
    ANYTHING about ANYTHING"
I said
"ANYTHING about ANY"
I was
I was really
and uh
Megan said to me
she says
"like you do??"
"like YOU DO??"

and I

do I?
do I know anything about?

(she smiles and looks at the girls from very far away)

    (sudden, to #2) honey
    are you eating?
    are you eating, honey?
    you've gotten so skinny
    i didn't even recognize
    just as long as you're eating
    ok?
    ok
    . . . ok

(she gets a little self-conscious)

    now we want to see a win out there!
    today!
    win! win! win!
    lots of fans
    Big Fans
    longtime fans came out just to see you!
    how cool is that?
    right?
    so cool
    Frank texted me and I was like
    "I am In"
    so none of that
    none of that stuff with the Fusion
    let's see some uh some smart soccer today
    smart passing smart listening smart eyes
    I've seen so many games
    you have no idea
    so many Saturdays and tournaments and practices and

    And Megan's watching
    Megan is

    (sudden and distraught) oh
    oh no I

I for
oh shoot I
I forgot to
shoot
from the trunk
the trunk!
oh god
I'm sorry
I'm so sorry
I'm
I'm so so
it's not
ok ok I'll be back in a jiff
I just forgot to
ok
I'm sorry
ok
it's ok
it's ok

(Soccer Mom hurries off
   a long, long silence
   whistle)

LYDIA R. DIAMOND

Smart People

In this monologue, Jackson, an African-American surgical intern, is explaining the reason for his fatigue at the end of a date that has gone badly.

JACKSON: So here's what I do. I'm a surgeon. I've been study-ing to be a surgeon for the last eight years. That's not including all of the pre-meds in college. And I did well. Straight A's. It seems I have a natural proclivity for just about anything I do. You know a residency is a hazing, an endurance test. They put us on these crazy hours in emergency. It's just barfing, blood, crying babies, and boys trying to kill themselves via one another . . . We're supposed to pay our dues for a couple of years and then follow around a real surgeon. Who's supposed to teach me. Except they don't like me. We don't need to waste time deconstructing why the black guy can't get a decent mentor in Boston. Yeah, okay. So, every now and then I don't feel like being treated like Sambo that day, and I push back, just a little. So today I say . . . "No . . .

when I wrote that about that patient on that chart there that you're holding . . . it's because I knew what I was doing . . . and when that nurse came up behind me and called Doctor-Whoever-The-Fuck to come in and second-guess me, and he decided that I'm sucky and so arbitrarily prescribed some kind of bullshit course of action . . . And now the patient's worse, and you will not pin that on me . . ." It doesn't matter how I say it . . . I'm "angry" and "volatile" and "not good at working with others," so I get written up and have to do the whole fucking bedpan thing again. *(Beat)* So today, I went to work, to the emergency room and I worked for ten straight hours, then I went to my clinic and worked another six . . . Because someone has to take care of those people . . . And then I made your ass dinner. And you're trippin' because I tease you about hot sauce. I don't have time for that.

JACKIE SIBBLIES DRURY

Really

A black (or brown) woman takes pictures of her artist boyfriend's mom. As they jockey for a claim to him, they try to redefine themselves in the wake of his legacy. This is a play about grief, intimacy, and the difference between goodness and greatness seen through the lens of photography.

This speech happens at the end of the play, and is delivered to the Mother of Calvin, the artist. It is by far the most the Girlfriend has ever said to the Mother, and the most honestly she has said it. The Girlfriend is thinking as she speaks, and trying to figure out how to articulate the impossible, so it should take some time.

GIRLFRIEND:
Well.

Okay. So. This is totally stupid
But if I sit for more than like five seconds, because
   I start to think about,
Not even me, I start to think about like the world.
   Kind of?

And it's like
When I think about it for more than like five seconds
    I start to cry, but
Okay.
I know this is obvious, but like
life for most of the people in the world, for most of
    the people that have ever lived,
the lives that they lived were horrible.

Okay. I'm not.
Now, I'm not thinking about it.
Like I'm actually not thinking about that anymore.
Like.
Okay.
So.
I don't know what we do.
It's like as soon as I go from outside of myself
to think about anyone but myself
Like, if I try to care about anyone but myself suddenly
    it's a thing that goes from a Me
to a We
and it's a problem for some vague group. That I'm
    not even sure I'm a part of.
Like oh, what am I going to make for dinner, but
    what do We do about the world?
How can I live without Calvin, but what do We do
    about the world?
What We, you know?
How can I make my art but what do We do . . .
It's like.

I think art is important.

Like, really, I do.

But maybe I only think it's important
because it's the thing that I come the closest to
    knowing how to do.

But even that.
I look at my work and I look at Calvin's work and
    I know,
that his is just better than mine.
I can't not look at his photos.
I am drawn into them. I want to look at them.
And I love him. And maybe that's why.
I don't know why, but they're just better.
And they've always been better
and people have always told us his were better, always
and that used to make me love him more.
And be So Jealous.
And so deeply in love.
At least I thought I was.
And Now
I don't know what to do with that.

And I feel bad for myself.

And then I think about my problems with respect to
    the world and I think, fuck.
And then I'm just thinking about myself again.
And thinking about him again.
And thinking about him not thinking about me.
Looking directly at me and not thinking about me at
    all.

And that's not uncommon.
It's not an uncommon thing to be alone. Or unhappy.
Or to want something that you don't get.
It's not uncommon to fail and fail and fail.
But when I look at Calvin's work and I look at my
    work I just I think, at least.
At least I know no one will remember anything of me.
At least I know that. At least I know that I'll never be
    recognized as anything
because I'll never make anything for anyone to see.

So that I'm not
I don't know
polluting the future.
Or something.

LAURA EASON

The Undeniable Sound of Right Now

It's 1992. Chicago. Hank is struggling to keep his legendary rock club going amid changing times and changing tastes. But when his beloved daughter, Lena, starts dating a rising star DJ, Hank must contend with the destructive power of The Next Big Thing.

HANK: I am jealous. That's a parent's prerogative. You spend your time with other people, with him. I like when you're here. I wish I didn't frankly. It would make my life a hell of a lot easier if I didn't give a rat's ass about you. But I do. I didn't think I would. I was too young to be a dad. I thought, what am I doing?! I'm not going to love this kid. But I did. From the first second. I loved you so much it made me mad. I keep thinking I'll get over it. For years, I've been hoping, "Okay, when she can sit up, I'm not going to be so attached. Okay, when she can talk, when she can walk. Okay, when she's ten and like a little person, I will not feel this. Okay, when she's sixteen, when she's twenty-one." Twenty-one—finally! I was so happy last year because you were a full-fledged adult and

I could get shot one night and know you'd be fine. But mostly because I wouldn't love you so much anymore. I could go back to the way it was. Because I never wanted to love something so much. I wanted to be connected to the earth loosely. Lightly. But, no, you came along and I was fucking tethered to it. No fucking up. No checking out. But last year, I said, "Okay, I can fuck up again. Check out if I want." But no, I can't. Because I can't stop loving you so goddamned much. Because there's no one else in my life I love as much as you, ever loved as much as you.

LARISSA FASTHORSE

What Would Crazy Horse Do?

A dark comedy in one act. Twin siblings, Journey and Calvin, are facing extinction. After the passing of their grandfather, they have become the last two of their tribe. Since their traumatic childhood they have promised to live womb to tomb, ending their lives together so neither is the last on the planet. Possibility has come knocking in the form of the new Ku Klux Klan who has realized that racial preservation is something both sides can get behind. After being mistakenly arrested, Calvin realizes that there is nothing left for them to fight for.

CALVIN: Tonight when the agents were taking us out of the clinic, all I could think of was you and your stupid meme. So I yell, "This is what Crazy Horse would do!" and I fight. The Indians all cheered and I felt fucking great as they wrestled me into the car. Then this huge Fed looks me straight in the eye and says, "Who the fuck is Crazy Horse?" It was like he grabbed my heart with his fist. Then the guy leans in and says, "Is Crazy Horse the ring leader?" I said, "He's the greatest Lakota war chief in history. He defeated Custer. They're carving the world's largest monument in his honor." He says, "Too bad, could have cut yourself a deal."

I rode alone in the back of that car and shit got simple. Everything in my life has been focused on meaning something to the world and I thought you screwed it up by going crazy. But in that car I realized we've been fighting all our lives against an enemy that doesn't even know we exist. We've already been mowed down and forgotten. We're mulch. We lost before we were even born. I swore if I ever got back to you, I'd never let you go again. We do it tonight. On our terms, together forever. Womb to tomb.

HALLEY FEIFFER

I'm Gonna Pray for You So Hard

David—a famous playwright in his early seventies—is talking to his daughter Ella, an up-and-coming actress in her twenties. They sit in their large but gone-to-seed Upper West Side apartment, drinking wine and smoking cigarettes. He is ranting about critics.

DAVID: See that's what I'm talking about—they're all fucking idiots—

No you *don't* know, Ella! Let me finish—they are a sick cadre of pathetic, sniveling, *tiny* men with *micropenises* and *no* imaginations who write out of their asses and who *love* to tear you down because in truth they know that you are doing *exactly* what they could never do—that you are doing the only thing they have ever *wanted* to do— and they are fucking *jealous*. You know that, don't you? How jealous they are? They're *boiling* with envy. They want a *piece* of you. They want in. They wanna get *inside* you! They wanna *climb right in!*

I'm *serious.* They wanna *fuck* you. They wanna fuck you so hard, they're *blind* with fuck-rage. And even though they're almost exclusively queers—you think that matters? It doesn't matter! Because the kind of fucking they wanna do to you is gender-blind, soul-blind—they're blind to it themselves! I mean it's like a fucking snot-nosed kid dipping your braid in his *inkwell*! They get a kind of pleasure out of being *perverse*.

I'm not kidding. Why are you laughing? It's like a pedophile and his *prey*! Humbert Humbert and Lolita! She obsesses him and this disgusts him so he abuses her and then he *fucks* her, and then abuses her and then *fucks* her again!

I mean haven't you realized it's always the *brilliant* performances that are the ones that go unnoticed—or even worse!—the ones that get the kind of condescending, bullshit mentions like: "The *serviceable* Ella Berryhill." "The capable . . ." "The reliable. . ." "The sturdy. . ." As if you're a fucking *stool* they enjoyed *sitting* on for the evening!

Or even worse: just the name, in *parentheses*—"When Medvedenko professes his love to Masha"—and then in parentheses: "(Ella Berryman)"—

Oh God, and *then*! What's even *worse*! Just to rub some salt in the wound—just really *grind* it in—after giving you the requisite, dismissive nod—"Ella Berryman" (close paren)—*then*, a paragraph later they'll say: "Well, the *real* pleasure of the evening is the *exquisite* performance of—"

And then they pick the *one person* in the cast who's a fucking *hack*! The one actor who's chewing the scenery as if he just got fucking *dentures* and he's getting executed next *Tuesday*!

Or the *"ingénue"*—the girl who's sexy, or (maybe more accurately), what a gay man thinks he's *supposed* to think is sexy—

Exactly! Like that fucking *Clementine* in your play! Your perfect little "Nina" . . .

But that's exactly what they *want*! A wide-eyed, little brain-dead . . . *trout*-mouth who clearly only a man *terrified* of his own mor*tality* would want to fuck!

LINDSEY FERRENTINO

Ugly Lies the Bone

Kelvin, a man too comfortable in his own skin, tells the following story to impress his girlfriend's sister. It doesn't work.

KELVIN *(As if he's the funniest man alive)*: I have a crazy life. I got two Aunt Kathys! One on each side. What're the odds? Two Uncle Jeffs, both married in. And three cousins named Frank, I mean what in the hell?! *There's big Frank, middle Frank, little Frank, my dad's cousin, my cousin, my cousin's son.* You with me? I'm textin', I'm textin' *all* the time, if you know me, y'know I'm textin' like a—I don't know what—textin' *all the Franks* the night a the NFL draft, we're lunatics, go to the games together, whatever. *So I text Frank* 'bout the Dolphin's number-one pick, which is just like COME ON!—*total* mistake. Follow football, football fan? Weeeeell, I text, "Let the shitty decisions begin." Meanwhile doesn't go to middle Frank, goes to LITTLE Frank, who is proposing to his girlfriend. Down on one knee and, "Let the shitty decisions begin!!" HA! Oh, oh. You'll love this! *All* the Franks're always forwardin' me emails, and I write back to *middle* Frank who I *think* is my cousin, all caps locks, I write, STOP SENDIN' ME RACIST REPUBLICAN BULLSHIT! We talk like that, we kid around, ya know. But instead it goes to *big* Frank, my dad's cousin, who is just like, not cool with it . . . *Hilaaaarious.*

LEIGH FONDAKOWSKI

Spill

On April 20, 2010, the BP-owned oil rig Deepwater Horizon
*exploded, killing eleven, and sending millions of barrels of oil into
the Gulf of Mexico, the largest environmental disaster in U.S. history.
Crafted from hundreds of interviews with those closest to the event
and its aftermath, this play explores where we are as a society and
illustrates the true human and environmental costs of oil.*

*Keith Jones, fifties, is a Southern lawyer who lost his son
Gordon on the* Deepwater Horizon *oil rig.*

KEITH JONES: I think about Gordon all the time. But last night
I couldn't go to sleep. I just couldn't go to sleep for thinking about Gordon's last moments on that rig. Nobody
knows what those last moments were like so imagination
creates lots of things. People say, "Don't think about it."
Well, it's not that easy, wish it was. One thing I've learned
is the Bible does not say that money is the root of all
evil. It says the love of money is the root of all evil. And
the love of money gave rise to a lot of bad greedy decisions—but see, my anger comes not from that Gordon

was killed, and not that he was killed because they were negligent, even though they were, and not even because they one by one took away all the different protections that existed on that rig, protections against a blowout until a point where a blowout was inevitable, had to happen and did happen—not even that. What makes me mad is that they did it for money. BP's reached the point where they've gotten their stockholder's money back. I don't have Gordon back. None of us have Gordon back, and all the money in the world won't get him back. Their business decisions took Gordon from us. And I don't care what kind of businessmen they are, they can't make it right for us. BP has not—even to this day—said, "We're sorry that you lost your son." *(Beat)* I guess fathers and mothers have said this for as long as children have been killed in coal mines and working on railroads, and in industry, and on the high seas, and our message never seems to be heard. *(Beat)* If you're gonna gamble your money, gamble your money. Take a risk with your business, that's fine. Don't gamble with people's lives, with children's dads. Don't gamble when you can't afford to cover your bet.

MADELEINE GEORGE

The (curious case of the) Watson Intelligence

Watson: trusty sidekick to Sherlock Holmes; loyal engineer who built Bell's first telephone; unstoppable super-computer that became reigning Jeopardy! champ; amiable techno-dweeb who, in the present day, is just looking for love. When Watson is hired by Merrick (small-town libertarian politician) to follow his ex-wife, Eliza (robotics engineer working on a start-up to solve the world's problems with artificial intelligence), a time-jumping technopolitical love triangle ensues. In this monologue, which ends Act I, Merrick begins by giving his stump speech for City Auditor, and transforms before our eyes into the Victorian version of himself, presenting the new smart-weapon he has invented to potential investors at a gentlemen's club in London.

> *(Lights warm on Merrick, facing out, in his office, after hours.*
> *He grooms himself in an unseen mirror, preparing to speak at a campaign event. Over the following, he combs his hair, adjusts his shirt, puts on and ties his red politician's necktie.)*

MERRICK: What I'm feeling right now is a tremendous— What Americans feel right now is a tremendous sense that their freedoms have been curtailed. Better word. Amputated. Better. Macheted. Macheted through the *neck*. Americans feel that our freedoms have been macheted through the *neck* by a government bent on taxing us to the hilt for what, for what?

To support a zombie army of "public servants" living at our expense, siphoning off the the the *life* juice that folks like you and I produce with our own hands. We're out there working, building things, making things happen, while they sit around with their feet up on desks that *we* paid for, barely putting in eight-hour days, just watching their pensions get fatter and fatter. As long as we keep ourselves plugged into this system, we the taxpayers will get weaker and weaker, while the so-called "servants" grow stronger and stronger. As Ayn Rand says, "The man who speaks to you of sacrifice is speaking of slaves and masters, and intends to be the master." One of my all-time favorite quotes.

(Continuously, as he speaks, Merrick begins undoing his necktie, unbuttoning his shirt, disorganizing his hair. He begins to groom himself to present at the Upperton Club in Pall Mall. He re-combs his hair in the Victorian style, re-buttons his collar, puts on and ties an ascot-style necktie.)

And that's why I'm running on a platform of total, and complete, individual, liberty. Total and complete independence for every citizen of this once-free nation. Now, I know true independence can feel harsh, especially at first. It can be a real *(He gestures: fist to his heart)*, I get it, I've been there. But it's either tear ourselves free from this system or die mangled in its gears, my fellow Americans! Sometimes the only way to achieve independence is to destroy the thing you're dependent upon.

(Merrick is fully Victorianized.
   He takes a breath.)

It is a pet theory of mine that you may know a man by the tools he uses, as well as by the tools he does not use. An example: I keep the points on my draftsman's pencils sharp, whittled down as I work until the leads are mere nubs, scarcely long enough to grasp between thumb and forefinger. But the gum erasers on the ends I never touch. Viz, I am precise. I make marks only where I want marks to be, and I do not mark twice.

(From his jacket pocket, Merrick produces a revolver, gleaming clean. He holds it up for his audience to see.)

Gentlemen, the tool I present to you today. From a distance it may look familiar, but its interior—you will have a moment to examine it more closely after I conclude—is revolutionary. It features, in its firing chamber, the miniature greaseless piston I have been seven years at perfecting. This mechanism is wedded to a calculating machine, a difference engine like Babbage's, but tiny and of my own design, enabling the tool to assess with precision many things we, with our clumsy brains, may only guess at. Targeting. Adjustment. Recoil. Sights. Viz, it is a perfect modern instrument. A weapon that knows more, in some ways, than its wielder.

If this instrument intrigues you, gentlemen, let me assure you that it pales in comparison to my even newer device, still too unfinished for public display. An object beyond objects, this new tool—once touched—will so exert its charms on you that you will never want it far from your hand. The prototype for this very advanced object is currently confined to my private workshop, but the day will soon come when I will reveal it, and usher in a dazzling new era of diminutive mechanization.

I conjure for you a future peopled with miniature machines, in every room of the home, on every street corner and in every shop. Noiseless doors that operate from yards away at the touch of a hydraulic button. Coal-fired hinge-mounted knives that may chop an entire bushel of apples in under an hour. A personal valet made of rivets and plates, whose brass caress, as he fits a man into his jacket, is a thousand times more sure than any boy's could ever be. In an insecure world filled with disloyal people, might we not finally find peace in this Mechanical Garden of Eden, where perfect servants greet us at every turn? What else may be mechanized, sirs, when such devices become commonplace? Where else in the world may we behold this new perfection?

Everywhere around us, gentlemen. Everywhere around us.

(Merrick slips the revolver smoothly into the inside pocket of his coat. He turns, then heads upstage into the dark.)

SARAH GUBBINS

Cocked

Attorney Taylor and her journalist girlfriend Izzie live a comfortable life in Andersonville. Their apartment, relationship, and strong anti-gun beliefs are shattered when Taylor's troubled brother Frank crashes, uninvited, into their lives. As secrets rise to the surface, the line between self-defense and safety is blurred.

In this monologue, Frank and his sister Taylor have just physically wrestled each other when Frank threatens to tell Izzie about the ongoing affair Taylor is having with a co-worker. Sent to cool off, nursing a lump on his head, Frank attempts to make amends with Taylor.

FRANK: I never got why people wanted the kinda life that you and Izzie have. The apartment. And all the stuff. I mean look at Mom and Dad. Like who would want that. Spending your life with someone you just started hating more and more every day. Like that was just being a tool. Just a recipe for disaster. But then, God, I don't know how to say this . . .

So I'm taking these classes at the community college, right?

And one day I'm in the cafeteria. And there's this girl.

I know, go ahead and roll your eyes. But this was different. She wasn't like super hot. She was pretty. Beautiful. She was definitely beautiful.

It's just that I couldn't breathe. I sat down at an empty table. I was shaking. I thought I was going to be sick. And then she just sat down across from me, and was like, "Hi. I'm Melissa. Are you in my chem class?" And of course I wasn't. But it broke the ice. I could only nod and smile. Like some fucking jamoke.

Right off she mentioned a fiancé. And man, that just crushed me. I had a girlfriend too, but it was just a seasonal thing.

We ended up talking for like an hour. And the same thing happened the next week. We meet in the caf. And then the next week. And the next. And it got to be that I was living for Wednesdays. Like I had to do laundry and everything. I never took her number. Or her email. 'Cause she had a guy and all. And then the semester was over. And I guess it never dawned on me, our schedules were going to change. And that next Wednesday I'm in the caf all alone. And it just sucked. I got some double-nachos, but didn't touch them.

Fast-forward. A week ago. I'm in the parking lot heading home. And I run into her. And she totally hugs me. Like a real hug not a church hug. And she's telling me about the wedding plans. They rented the Radisson. And lined up Cancun for the honeymoon. And I'm like dying inside. There's this voice in my head going, "Kiss her, dude. Do it now!" And then she's making this move to go, 'cause it is cold out. And she does that thing, she says, "So good to see you, Frank." And she says my name. Like I've never heard it said. And all of a sudden I don't want to just kiss her anymore. That's not even close. That's not gonna be enough. I see the whole thing flash in front of me. Dates, drive-ins, kids, pumpkin patches. Christmas lights. Matching sweaters. Picking out our own snow blower. That whole thing. All the shit I've always hated. I wanted it. With her.

But there is no universe where she should pick me. I'm an ex-con. I've stolen from every job I've ever had. You know me. The dumb fuck. There's no way a girl like that, like Melissa, should ever be with a guy like me. Ever. And it's not like I think people ever really get a second chance. But I don't know. I just got sick of it. So I packed it in. Gave Terrell the rest of my AutoZone shit. He gave me three eight balls of coke to deliver to his cousin for cash. And I got on a bus. Showed up here. 'Cause at a certain point you get tired of being a fuck-up.

(Beat.)

But you're not a fuck-up. And I guess. I guess I just think you have a chance at something with Izzie and I don't want you to blow it. Over something stupid.

DIPIKA GUHA

I Enter the Valley

I Enter the Valley *is a play about a (fictional) great poet Augusto Reál and the women who enter his life at a moment when he has acute writer's block. It is a play about the nature of love, creativity, and aging. This monologue is from the play's second act: "Writing." Magdalena, Augusto's oldest mistress and caretaker, has had her house overrun by women, the youngest of whom has just been revealed to be pregnant. In this moment Henna, Augusto's glamorous first wife, tells Magdalena about the first moment she encountered her and what her presence has meant in her life.*

HENNA: You know, when you first walked into our lives . . . when you first walked in the door, I thought you were the most elegant woman I'd ever seen in my life, myself included, so that's saying something. I was running around trying to have influence, starting fires . . . when he left I . . . I couldn't understand it. I gave the best parties, could hold my own with prime ministers . . . I loved being part of everything just like him. Who else, I thought, could do that with him? So I came back here to see. It was just after he left. I drove myself. I wanted to see if I could talk some sense into him. He was there at the door when I arrived. He said you were out for a walk, and he was worried you'd be back any minute, so he made me hide. I was furious, so I hid very badly in here behind the curtain— I mean very badly—you could see my shoes sticking out. And then I looked out the window. The sky was light blue but the moon was very full and high and then I saw you, out in the garden looking at the peas, humming to yourself, in a white dress. You looked like you were hovering over the land. Like you were part of it and above it at the same time . . . like light.

And that's when I understood. He wasn't coming back. I've never . . . I've . . . and this is hard for me to say . . . I've had husbands but I've never really had . . . I tried to control everything all the time—especially him and look what happened. I didn't have the courage to just let things be. I have four houses, Magdalena, and I've never really lived in any of them. But your house . . . here, I'm at home.

KAREN HARTMAN

SuperTrue

Janelle is around forty. For the purpose of the monologue, any eth-nicity. Janelle, a city person, and her husband, Martin, have rented a summer cabin to try to relax and get pregnant. It's not working. Now Janelle is alone, talking to a child who appeared in the woods the night before. This child is portrayed by a puppet, but to Janelle she is real.

JANELLE: Do you know the story of Hannah? Samuel, chapter one?

Hannah's mouth could not make the words for what she wanted.

Hannah came to the temple and she curled in a little ball on the ground, and she tried to say, I am love, I am unbounded love, my name means grace—allow me a child to love.

She tried to say, my parents are dead and my sister is far. I must increase love.

She tried to say, I am empty, I am open, I am a vessel. Lend me someone who needs me.

But she was so tangled, her yearning so vast, that the sound for baby came out fucked up, maybe like: A BAAAYAH.

And love was something like: A LAYYYA.

And maybe kindness and need and her missing sister were: AAIIII. A MEEEEEEENA. Abkadlo go rono man mamamamamamamamamaKILIBAKAMAIII.

Until even the nonsense tangled in her chest, and snot ran down her face, and Hannah blubbered into the mucus, "Let me love."

And the priest threw her in the drunk tank, this crazy lady who ditched her niece's first birthday party, who walks a block out of her way to avoid a playground, this lady who took a prenatal yoga class because her doctor said being near pregnant women stimulates hormones, but then at the end of the class the mommies all sang to the babies inside them, and said how many weeks, and she yelled, "Seven," and ran out the building and down the block and hailed a taxi to a neighborhood where nobody knew her, and got drunk at a bar in the middle of the day. And might have kissed a man who was not her husband. And considered sleeping with this man, but did not.

Because even in her reverse grief for the unspooled future, Hannah knew that loving more includes loving well. That she could not break her bond.

Hannah festered. She bargained: "Give me this child and I will raise him to serve you." Meaning, I will not hoard love.

The bargain worked. She birthed a boy and kept her word. Samuel became a great leader, a righteous person, and a judge. And Hannah rejoiced even though the boy lived at the monastery because when she read her Bible at night when her husband couldn't see, and came to the part where God promises Abraham to number his descendants like the stars in the sky, Hannah knew one of those stars was for her.

All Hannah wanted was to shine with the rest of the sky.

(Pause.)

So now I use a clothesline. I eat low on the food chain. I bicycle to the market with sacks on my back.

Because I don't yet know the terms of my bargain. But I am ready. To break with habit. To consume less and give more.

You picked the right house.

AMINA HENRY

Bully

Both Bree and Delilah discover that they have been victims of random beatings. Bree suspects the women in their mutual aerobics class as being the perpetrators and invites Delilah to her apartment to discuss what they should do. Bree and Delilah bond over doughnuts and whiskey.

DELILAH: I used to get teased a lot in high school. I'm not sure why, I guess there was just something about me. I was really shy, I didn't know how to talk to people, or how to dress, I was on the honor roll. My mother was gone a lot so I had to figure out some stuff on my own. "Delilah is a dyke cunt fuck fat bitch suck it." I remember that one. It was written in the last stall of the third-floor girls' bathroom. I used to go to that stall on purpose, just to look at it. I don't know why, because it always made me feel like shit. And I never did anything. I never said anything. I just carried that label around. "Dyke cunt fuck fat bitch suck it." That was me until I graduated. I'd sit at home watching *Saturday Night Live* and eating pints of ice cream. Forget about the prom. I never even had a date until I got to college . . . It wasn't all bad. I had some nice teachers. And I played the flute in the orchestra. I liked playing the flute. I'm not really in contact with the people I went to high school with now. Just on Facebook. A lot of the kids I knew are fat now.

(Bree takes a drink.)

I still spend a lot of Saturday nights watching *Saturday Night Live* and eating ice cream by myself. Frozen yogurt now. But yes, I'm a lawyer. I was able to buy my mother a condo. And I have a lot of sex. Usually on Mondays. There's a guy I met on the internet. So—yeah.

LAURA JACQMIN

Residence

The play centers around Maggie, a new mom just heading back to her job as a medical supply saleswoman after an extended leave. After checking into an extended-stay hotel in Tempe, Arizona, for a month-long sales trip, she finds herself forming a close friendship with hotel front-desk clerk Bobby, a stoner with swagger and his own misgivings about parenthood. As Maggie decompensates and her depression returns—abandoning her meds in favor of self-medication—her backstory begins to come clear. This monologue takes place during the climactic scene of the play, on the roof of the hotel. Maggie pushes Bobby too far when she claims to be making plans to move to Tempe. When he reminds her of her responsibilities at home, she jabs back, pointing out that he left his own kid. When he accuses her of using what he did to "fuck up her own life," this is her response.

MAGGIE: My husband had me involuntarily committed because he caught me trying to drown Jamie in the sink. He had to punch me twice in the side of the head and lock me in the trunk of our Corolla to get me to stop fighting.

I was in the hospital for six weeks.

Every single one of the twenty-three days I've spent at home since then, Ben has slept with Jamie in a locked room that I'm not allowed into.

(Beat.)

He won't leave me alone with him.

(Beat.)

And why would he? Right?
      'Cause I've gotta say . . .
      When I had the sink full, and I had Jamie on that "Afternoon Tea Time" dish towel, and he was looking up at me, that open little face, that tiny little blank, and I scooped him up, one hand under his back, the other supporting his head, and I started to sliiiide him down underneath—
      It felt like the rightest thing in the world to do.
      Like the *only* thing.
      Like if I just did that . . .
      Everything else would come into focus.

(Beat.)

I *miss* that feeling. Even though I *know* that feeling is . . .

(She can't finish—it's too enormous. Then:)

So, I'm moving to Tempe.
      What else am I supposed to *do*. Right?

(Beat.)

Unless I just kill myself.
      It doesn't—*feel* like something I would do?
      But.
      I don't really know *what* I do anymore.

HANSOL JUNG

Cardboard Piano

Northern Uganda on the eve of the millennium. Chris, the daughter of American missionaries, and Adiel, a local teenage girl, steal into a darkened church to seal their love in a secret, makeshift wedding ceremony. But when the surrounding war zone encroaches on their fragile union, they cannot escape its reach. Confronting the religious and cultural roots of intolerance, Cardboard Piano *explores violence and its aftermath, as well as the human capacity for hatred, forgiveness, and love.*

> *(Sixteen-year-old Chris has packed her bags with plans to flee town with Adiel, after a disastrous coming-out session to her parents. Adiel shows resistance to the escape plan, launching Chris into the following plea.)*

CHRIS: They're leaving! Moving boxes, plane tickets,
    Really Leaving Adiel. With *me.*
    I had to tell them, they are these people who are supposed to love me the most in the world

I thought maybe they would, understand, thought they'd—

But it went wrong, okay, it just went wrong and, Adiel, if we are gonna do this, each other is all we're gonna have left—we have to put everything on the line.

I mean EVERYTHING.

I have to put my God on the altar, you have to put your country on the altar, and say, none of these things matter more to us than each other, each other is our everything, for each other we are willing to burn them destroy them to to to give them up whatever "them" is for either of us. You know that game, that game where they ask you, if you were stranded on an island, and you get to take just the one thing, what would you take? Except it's not a game, we *are* stranded on an island, we are all stranded on an island on our own, and we get to choose one thing just the one thing that we will carry with us always.

My parents chose God, your parents chose country, and look what happened to them!

Mine are forced to box up their house and dreams in a weekend, yours are dead.

I can't do that, I can't be stranded on an island on my own,

I *choose you.* But it only works if you choose me too.

No More Sad Things

Jessiee, a thirty-two-year-old woman, takes a last-minute flight to Maui to escape her life in Akron, Ohio. There she meets a local stranger, Kahekili, on Kā'anapali Beach. They flirt. They have sex. Then as the sun rises she learns that the stranger is fifteen years old. Meanwhile a wily, playful and ukulele-wielding Guidebook helps us navigate through the slippery exploration of how stories linger in the body.

(Kahekili returns home after his chance meeting with the haole [not-Hawaiian] lady on the beach and absolutely denies his wish to be able to connect with his drunk father.

Spoken in Hawaiian pidgin:)

KAHEKILI:

> Haw, bruh, I get home t'row my board up against da wall
> an tek some ice for dis my *ule*.
> Li'dat, my little man, I wen rub him up against some serious grains a sand nuh,
> buggah be purple!
> UGH
> Shoots, bruh, da ocean, she always ready wid some new kine da painful stuff.
> But I love dis.
> My purple penis, neh?
> Da hurt mek you into somet'ing else nah?
> Y'scrap some, y'bleed some,
> an da blood from da scrap, get you goin, get you harder, get you stronger
> Till you know you strong enough fo' tek off da shirt an scrap wid da big bruddas out deh.
> NAH? NAH? ha.
>
> Ye, deh I stay wid dis pack a frozen broccoli rollin over my *ule*,
> My fadda come home wid a new pile a scrap wood and da stink a death on his face
> We don't even talk now, not even.
> Li'dat, he see his dinner on his boy's balls an he just pass on by, li'dat.
> Jus' li'dat.
> Pass on by.
>
> Shoots brah, like I wanna talk with him, neh?
> Nah. Forget about it.

Wolf Play

An adopted Korean boy is ushered into a new home by his adopted American father. The American father un-adopts the boy by a single signature on a piece of paper. This new home belongs to an American boxer and her wife. But just before the boy leaves for the new home, his ex-father finds out that the new couple, to whom he has "re-homed" his ex-son, is a lesbian couple. The American ex-father spends the rest of the play trying to get the boy back.

The Korean boy is a puppet, puppeteered by a Wolf, who begins the play with this speech:

WOLF: What if I said I am not what you think you see.

    I am not an actor human, this floor is forest earth, and to the left of that glaring exit light, a river flows, the width and length and velocity of the Egyptian Nile.

    You are not what you feel you are, you are a spider the size of your eyelash. Or an eagle flying two thousand feet above our heads. Or the mother of the newest freshest pinecone dangling over that aisle. We are riding on the back of a giant turtle, hurtling through the cosmos, in a four-point-five four-billion-year race against the tiniest of the tiniest white Easter rabbits.

    What if I said, you are the single most important breath in my space. You are the first gear that turns the clock of my world. You are the final drop of dew that breaks down the universal dam of miscommunication. I need you with every blood cell and cranial nerve I possess.

    And you believed me?

    Does that change anything?

    What if I said Oops, actually no, we are sitting in a rented space on top of concrete ground, laid upon a planet fast losing her steam. You are barely a breath in the time-space continuum, you're here, you're gone, we'd all move on without a care. You do not make an impact, you do not give or take anything of import in your ridiculous little life on this plastic earth.

I am exactly what you think you see. I am indeed an actor human, paid in cash or credit or So Much Love and cookies to say these lines that a writer human wrote so that I might speak them in my actor human-resonant voice: You are indeed the idiot that decided to pay to be squeezed in that little seat in the dark, for the next some hours of your life that you shall never retrieve, you may not take pictures or recordings, you must silence all cell phones beepers candy wrappers alarm clocks and all alarmedness in general, or we will tweet about you and your ignorance to the entire world during our greenroom smoke break, and you are exactly what you feel you are.

That is the truth. Is that the truth?

You may think about this while some people are turning the noisy things off.

Go on.

(People turn noisy things off.)

The truth is a wobbly thing, we shall wobble through our own set of truths like jello on a freight train, and tonight I add a bump to that journey and put to you my truth:

I am not what you think you see.

I am the wolf.

Aow.

Yes, I am the wolf.

Aooow.

And then again because three translates to God in the bible, infinity in Asia, and funny in theater:

I am the wolf.

(Real wolf howl. Terrifying and beautiful.)

MJ KAUFMAN

Sagittaruis Ponderosa

Sagittarius Ponderosa *tells the story of Archer, a twenty-nine-year-old transboy, moving home to the forests of central Oregon to take care of his sick father. This scene occurs after Archer's father, Pops, learns from his doctor about a Jewish custom in which people who are very sick take a new name so that the Angel of Death won't be able to find them. Even though he is not Jewish, Pops decides to go through his own version of this ritual.*

POPS: I want to do it my way. It's for me.

On this day November 28th, I will be taking a new name.

I will no longer be just Robert. Which is a name that has served me well. And has given me many other names. Including Rob, Robby, and Robo-cop. And means bright glory. And is the name of many an important leader, scientist, artist, and otherwise important figure throughout history. And gave me my primary moniker since the age of ten which has been Bob. A one-syllable name, which I always liked. Because you can say it quickly. And it always made me think of bobbing for apples. Bending with a distinct goal and popping back up again. After getting splashed with water.

Basically, it's all served me very well.

My new name will be Robert Jason. Jason, means health, healer, healing. Jason is the one who sought the golden fleece. Jason is two syllables and slides around in your mouth in a kind of satisfying way.

At least I think so. You're the ones that will be saying it a lot.

So. Let's practice. Let's all go around and practice calling me by my new name.

NAMBI E. KELLEY

Native Son

Chicago, the South Side, 1930s. A world where opportunity is elusive for people like Bigger Thomas. After landing a job in the home of a wealthy family, Bigger unwittingly unleashes a series of events that violently and irrevocably seal his fate. Using W. E. B. Du Bois's theory of double consciousness as a grounding point, this adaptation of Native Son *focuses on the landscape inside the mind of Bigger Thomas, bringing the power of Richard Wright's novel to life for a whole new generation.*

In this speech, the Black Rat, Bigger's alter ego, tries himself in the court of his mind, assuming the voices of the witnesses questioning his own innocence in the death of Mary Dalton.

(The Black Rat and Bigger are alone. The Black Rat encircles Bigger, antagonizing him, as the voices of the witnesses murmur behind him in darkness.)

THE BLACK RAT *(As Mrs. Dalton)*: "Yes, that's the Negro boy who came to my home to work."

(As Buddy) "Yeah, we used to steal from stores and newsstands."

(As Mr. Dalton) "Yes, that's the earring in the furnace we'd given to Mary."

(As Britten) "Yes, his fingerprints were found on the door of Miss Dalton's room."

(As Hannah) "Yes, my son is a low-down dirty rat! But he ain't no killer, nuh uh."

(As Jan) "Yes, I shook hands with the Negro. He is a human being after all."

(As Gus) "Yeah that fool kicked me the morning we planned to rob Blum's!"

(As Bessie) "Yes, he clubbed me multiple times with a brick and dumped me down that nasty air shaft! I tried to climb out but I-I-I-I froze to death. See?! The dead body of Bessie Mears!"

(Flashbulbs flash. The Black Rat reveals Bessie's dead, naked, frozen body. Flashbulbs flash.)

"The bones of Mary Dalton!"

(Flashbulbs flash. Mary's bones are on a table. Gasps. Sobs from courtroom members. Suddenly, the Black Rat grabs Mary's decapitated skull, manipulating it like a puppet, and making her sing. To Bigger's ear, it's Mary's voice singing:)

> Coming fer to carry me home
> Swing low, sweet chariot
> Coming fer to carry me home.

You're guilty!
Am I—?

GEORGETTE KELLY

Ballast

Ballast *tells the story of two relationships between transgender and cisgender partners, exploring not only the way gender influences our relationships, but also how gender seeps into our spirituality, our dreams, and our ability to take flight. Grace is a transgender woman who wants to return to her calling as a pastor after a leave of absence. Her wife, Zoe, is struggling with Grace's recent transition, revealing the fault lines of their marriage.*

> *(Zoe and Grace are in bed together.*
> *Grace sits up.)*

GRACE:

> Dreams stress me out.
> They always have.
> When I can remember them—which isn't always—
>   they are
> disjointed, disheartening, dysphoric:
> the tone always off, like a ringing in my ears,
> like a reminder I don't belong.

At first, Zoe was a talisman:
With her in my bed, I dreamed of nothing—
the nights were made of thick gray static,
and relief like living water.
But recently the dreams are back.

(A shift.
Grace finds herself in a dream.
She is at a stone pulpit.)

First, I would like to thank you for such a warm welcome
to your community.

(She hesitates.)

Joining a new church can be . . .

(She is paralyzed.)

Very daunting.

(Unseen voices start to boo.)

Especially when people are booing!

(Unseen people start to throw pieces of bread at her.)

And throwing communion bread at the pulpit!
Come on, people, stop it!

(They don't.
She picks up the communion chalice.
And chugs it.
She takes a flask out of her vestments.
Refills the communion chalice with liquor from the flask.
And chugs it again.
The bread rains down heavier.)

It's not like I'm asking anything of you, it's not like you think, it's not like the movies, it's not like I've been lying, it's not like I'm abandoning you, it's not like I'm the first, it's not like I'm the only, it's not like it's my fault.

(A shift.
Out of the dream.)

I wake tangled in sweaty sheets, but she doesn't notice.

BOO KILLEBREW

Miller, Mississippi

Miller, Mississippi *begins with a ghost story told to the Miller children by their family's black maid in 1960, and ends in 1994 after reality has proved far worse for this genteel Southern family. After Judge Jonathan Miller commits suicide in the family living room, deeply hidden secrets begin to ooze out of the walls. Mildred, the Miller matriarch, is desperate to prevent any further tragedy and lives in a state of denial, gin, and naps. Thomas, the eldest child, picks up where his father left off. Becky attempts to escape through visual art, as her trauma and surroundings begin to close in around her. In this speech, Mildred reveals why she has not stopped Thomas from preying upon his sister.*

MILDRED: I want you to listen to me. How do you think you're gonna get men other than your brother to dance with you or take you to balls? Becky. There is nothing else I can do for you. You have to become a lady. You have to flirt with society. You have to have a coming out, you have to eat food, you have to wash yourself, you have to stop sending letters and picture books to John, you have got to get out of this house. You have got to get out of this house. You have got to clean this plate and you have got to get out of this house. You have got to. You do something! Eat! You do something for yourself! I tried saving you once before, you know that? I told your father I was gone leave. I said, "I know what you're doing to her. I'm leaving. I'm taking her and I'm leaving." You know what happened after I said that? He blew his goddamn brains out! Because you needed saving!

If you think that I'm gone risk saving you again, you got another think coming. If you think that I'm gone try and stop Thomas only to have his goddamn brains splattered all over my carpet, you got another think coming. You have got to get out of this house. You have got to go to dances and you have got to find someone. You have got to find someone who is going to get you out of this house. Eat this goddamn food so you can fit into your goddamn dress. You save your goddamn self.

(Pause. The women look at each other.)

You have got to get out of this house and save yourself.

BASIL KREIMENDAHL

Orange Julius

After being poisoned by Agent Orange in the jungles of Vietnam, Julius is dying. Nut, his trans-masculine daughter, tries to reconnect with their father as one man to another by caring for his decaying body, sorting through childhood memories, and diving into war-movie fantasies. As worlds and identities blur, Nut reconciles with their gender and finds unexpected intimacy.

NUT: A year before my dad got sick it was my grandmother.

FRANCE: She keeps asking me to take her out with the garbage.

NUT: So she got the doctor to prescribe my grandmother anti-depressants, then my mom hid them in her brownies.

FRANCE: I can't stand it anymore.

NUT: She died in our house. In her bed. It was my mother who took care of her too. I helped to change her Depends once, and I said I love you for the first and last time.

When she died my mother was holding her face and wiping her mouth and telling her it was okay while she choked on the foam coming up from her lungs.

I wrote a song about it. The song was called "Lubee in Search of Her Feet." Because my grandmother had a giant round stomach and skinny legs. And I wondered if she wondered what her feet looked like as she laid in her bed.

Hospice came and brought her a wheelchair and a bed.

Hospice came and brought my dad a recliner and a bed.

FRANCE: Help me get your father into the bed.

KIMBER LEE

different words for the same thing

Thirteen years and eighteen hundred miles separate Alice from her childhood home. But after one phone call, the small-town streets and characters that once shaped her, come rushing back and threaten to never let her go. This monologue is spoken by Alice's adopted father, Henry, while he is alone onstage.

> *(A neighborhood on the south end called Mangum Heights.*
> *A modest, comfortable home.*
> *A well-used, tidy kitchen.*
> *It's possible there are kitchen-counter items and hand towels with happy chickens or geese on them. Maybe a happy chicken napkin holder on the table with matching salt-and-pepper shakers.*
> *A toolbox is open in the counter.*
> *Henry lifts the kitchen sink faucet—no water.*
> *He speaks while he works:)*

HENRY: It was because I was asked to fly Barney Beers to Eugene
and back
    for a choir concert.

Barney was the quarterback on our high school
football team and also the trumpet player for the
church's contemporary Christian jazz ensemble,
Sounds of Joy.
It's hard to find a good trumpet player.

(He fiddles with something under the sink.)

So anyhoo . . .
I said I'd fly him over there because at that time me
and some guys had a little Cessna, a one fifty
little nine one Juliet.
It's an easy hop to Eugene.
And while I was waiting in the vestibule there for
Barney to play his trumpet,
I saw a pile of brochures
and they had pictures of these kids in Korea
little faces little eyes.
And I
Barney and I flew home
and at the football game watching him quarterback
that night
it was fourth and long in the second quarter and I said
Marta
I said
I think we should adopt a Korean baby.
And she looked at me like I had dropped straight down
from Jupiter.
And I showed her the brochure.
And she looked at it and there was a
long pause.
Barney threw a bomb and found the Miller kid in the
end zone with three seconds left in the half.
And then Marta said
I'll pray about it
and
she did.

(He refastens something on the faucet, tries it—no water.)

That chat she had with God
I don't
I don't know as I'd say that was an easygoing
    conversation
more like it mighta been a
a uh
knockdowndragout type of deal.
Anyhoo . . .
We picked her up in Eugene
not flying this time.
My mother stayed with Maddy and we drove over.
She was so tiny and
silent
staring and blinking
no crying not a peep.
I thought it at the time and I think it now
I said it to Marta I said
How strange
Wouldn't you cry
if you had been plucked up from the place you knew,
    smells sounds sights
all taken from you
or you from them
and alone flown across an ocean with no memory.
I think you would cry.
I would.
And so when I held Alice for even that very first time
    I felt a
a uh
a high regard for her uh
for her uh
for the way she held herself even as a little tiny baby
instincts
like a good hunting dog
silent and watchful.

MARTYNA MAJOK

Ironbound

At a bus stop in a run-down New Jersey town, Darja, a Polish immigrant cleaning lady, is done talking about feelings; it's time to talk money. Over the course of twenty years, three relationships, and three presidents, Darja negotiates for her future with men who can offer her love or security, but never both. Ironbound *is a portrait of a woman for whom love is a luxury—and a liability—as she fights to survive in America. This unsentimental proposal is delivered to Darja by Tommy, her serially cheating boyfriend. Linda is the rich woman for whom he had left Darja. Aleks is Darja's troubled son.*

TOMMY: Billions of women, actually. There are actually billions of women out there. And maybe even close to a million just like you. I was just doin' that thing where I listen real well. Millions. Just like you. To choose from. But you see what I'm doin' here? *(He gets down on one knee)* I don't have a ring but do you see what I'm doin'? Look, I'm not a fuckin' stud, okay. I know that. I'm arright. But listen. And no I don't exactly make bank. But I pay my bills. And yeah I've fucked up. Fucked around.

Okay. But yer also not a model, sorry, and I still love the fuckin' shit outta you. Yer logic's aggravation, yer English is ridiculous, and you are one straight-up crazy fuckin'— yer crazy, D, sometimes. But you got wonderful legs. And yer heart is good. You like goin' to the movies. I *love* goin' to the movies. You need a car. I got a car. I can make you pasta. You could make me lunches. And it's good to know that someone's got the keys if I forget mine.

Darja. Aleks didn't get to choose. And he hasn't. He hasn't been. Choosin'. Lately. You.

I do. And I will. Every day. Fuckin' swear.

. . . Yes?

. . . No?

. . .

. . . Okay.

(Tommy gets off his knee.)

Okay. Okay, I'll just drop it. I guess you can forget it. Sorry. I don't even have a ring. Not even a fuckin' silver one. (The stores don't open—I just wanna say—not this early.)

I knew Linda would leave. I think. In my, like, heart. They always leave. Allison. Courtney. All of 'em. Eventually. I mean . . . stay. They never leave. They just stay where they always been and I gotta leave. I go home. But now yer not there. And it's so . . .

At least you tap my phone. Which is fucked, but. At least you gave a fuck enough about me to tap my phone. Which is something.

You know my mother's birthday. Backwards. Which is something.

I knew you'd be here. I knew that. Which, I think, is something . . . *(Dropping it)* Okay.

Petty Harbour

On the rocky shores of Petty Harbour, Newfoundland, a small house stands against a storm. A strange phone call brings three banished sons back to their childhood home, which has since been turned into a makeshift church by their father. The weather rages, the whiskey is opened, and the visitors that nobody expected will arrive. Petty Harbour *is a haunted mystery thriller and poetic family drama about pride, forgiveness, and being a woman with ambition in a world with certain expectations. After a few hours of drinking and fighting, Freddy, a family friend with a secret, warns the sons, Nolan and Dean, about their anger.*

FREDDY *(Newfoundland accent)*: When yer alone in yer house—ya ever come to wake alone in yer apartment? Or with someone? 'N' do ya look in her face 'n' find there's nothin'? The answer's not in her eyes either 'n' what are you to do now? Nor's it in a bottle. Or in Chicago. Or—or in just about anywhere ya look. 'N' do ya sit in silence sometimes 'n' wonder how you'll end? Wonder who'll tell stories of ya. Or if they even will. What's the point a ya, ya little man in yer little room, listenin' to the family ya rent from, laughin' 'n' movin' above ya 'n' ya wish ya didn't hate, ya wish. Ya look at yerself 'n' think . . . hardly any time's passed but already yer too old. What is the point of ya. What is the point of you indeed.

'N' then, right then's when he comes. Cuz the devil need only visit the good. Wouldn't we all rather ransack the *nice* houses. He'll walk right on in 'n' chew yer heart to crumbs, the devil is real. 'N' he'll leave nothin' of ya. Nothin'. That's when you'll hope you've said a kind word to someone. That's when you'll hope someone cares enough to find ya in yer little room, pull ya back from the ledge. That's when you'll wish ya forgave. People might fail you or hurt you terrible bad in this life. But if you blacken yer heart, Nolan, Dean, who'll find it in the dark? *(To Nolan)* Young Mister Murphy, *(To Dean)* Young Mister Murphy, ya gotta leave *some* light on.

MONA MANSOUR

Unseen

Conflict photographer, Mia, wakes up in the Istanbul apartment of Derya, her on-again, off-again girlfriend after being found unconscious at the scene of a massacre she was photographing. Mia can't even remember being there, but she wired photos of the site hours before she was found. The two women resume their volatile push-pull when Mia's well-meaning Californian mother arrives in Istanbul from the U.S., trying to help unravel what happened to her daughter. As we learn more about the incident itself, we also find out about some of the dynamics between all three women, and how they each navigate the difficulties of the worlds they encounter. Here, Jane, white, early sixties, finds herself alone with Derya, Turkish, early thirties. Both women are worried about Mia. In an attempt to try to understand her daughter, and calm herself down, Jane remembers a story from Mia's childhood.

JANE: There was always a part of her that was just drawn to the fragile things, you know. Or had a capacity for looking at them. God. I don't know. Maybe it seems to you we couldn't have had anything terrible to look at in our neck of the woods. Where Mia grew up. I mean, how do you measure these things? People's suffering. Is it measurable? Is it just about what each of us perceives to be suffering? I think about those things . . . We had a dog when Mia was, oh, seven or so. And he was, a rescue, and um, crippled or something from the start, and we did everything. German shepherds. They have this thing, it's—well it's part of their breeding. It's resulted in this hip thing, so, we got him the operation, and then animal physical therapy—they have that—and even a heating pad for him every morning. So he could walk, but it was always—just a funny walk—and, and people would see him and assume we were horrible people, and he was in pain, and why didn't we just put him to sleep. They'd say that. And Mia was always, just. She didn't care what anyone said. She said one time, and she had to have been no more than ten, she said, said to me after one of these people had offered their opinion again, she said, "It's hard for them to look at him because they're afraid for themselves." I mean, who is this kid? Can you believe she said that? I can't believe she said that. I always supported her doing this work because I thought, she could bear the cost of witnessing. And someone has to witness. You know? *(Having gotten emotional)* I'm sorry. I think I'm just a little exhausted.

MEG MIROSHNIK

The Tall Girls

Welcome to Poor Prairie, the dusty, desolate town where fifteen-and-a-half-year-old Jean has been exiled as caretaker for her wild-child cousin, Almeda. It's a grim, dangerous place to eke out an existence as a teenage girl—until a handsome man with a past arrives, a brand-new basketball in tow. As the town's girls come together to form a team set on making it out of Poor Prairie, a murky committee of townspeople threatens to stamp out girls sports altogether. Inspired by the flourishing and decline of high school girls basketball teams in the 1930s rural Midwest, The Tall Girls *asks: Who can afford the luxury of play? And what is the cost of childhood? This speech early in the play introduces Lurlene, the very tallest girl in town. In it, she talks to her best friend (the offstage Puppy, who is, as always, doing Lurlene's bidding) about her dreams of transcending their bleak surroundings.*

> *(Lights up on Lurlene, sixteen, standing onstage with a cigarette and a photograph. She wears a floral dress and flat shoes and is very, very tall. A shriveled-up old graying basketball lies next to her.*

As she talks, she plays around with the unlit cigarette, mimicking glamourous poses.)

LURLENE: She finally gave it to me, Puppy. After three solid years of humbling myself to my knees, donchaknow, Inez finally put it into my hands. And I been looking at Hazel Shoots' Downstate Tournament Royalty photograph like my eyes were gumstuck to it ever since. For the last six days, I have been painting my nails, bathing, and relieving myself with this image, that's how devoted I've been to Hazel's likeness.

And the thing I see is: Hazel Shoots was given *a tiara.* Hazel Shoots was *crowned* Queen of the Tournament. Never mind that she only made it out over to Humboldt to marry a player from the Humboldt boys team, because she got a *tiara.* Well, this leads me to the other bit I noticed in my study of Hazel Shoots' features, which is: *She isn't no better looking than me.*

For one, she has an inferior Cupid's bow. And still! She was given a tiara. Only think on what could've happened to me if I'da been old enough to go downstate with my superior Cupid's bow three years back. It was then I pulled out my old copy of *The Red Book*—you know the one with the photo of the Babe's Ballers inside. (I don't spend time on that picture, Babe Dublin looks like a sweaty wrestler in a wig.) No, I flip through the close-ups of starlets and socialites in satin and, again, do you know what I found?

There are plenty of starlets and socialites who don't look all that much better than Hazel Shoots, meaning that there are plenty who don't look half as good as me. So now I'm thinking to myself, Could be I should be in satin. To do that, I'd need to leave Poor Prairie. They're all wearing white in those photos and you know as well as me it's near unthinkable to keep white bleached and clean here. But what if I could leave Poor Prairie? (And not for trouble of the nine-month variety neither. Lord knows the girls who get sent away for a little less than a year . . . those girls certainly ain't wearing white.) No,

I gotta go somewhere where I could wear nail paint every day.

And donchaknow it was with that thought in my head that I answered the door this morning and saw Cyril Cosgrove standing there with his hat in his hand. I said: "Cyril, I don't mean to bust up your heart—I never wanted it to end this way—but I come to see that I am a better looker than not only former Tournament Queen Hazel Shoots—" (I showed him the photograph at that point, since I had it, like I been saying, handy.) "—but also a good number of the starlets and socialites in *The Red Book*, which leads me to say that I am not long for Poor Prairie. Which leads me to say that we are not long for our love. Please, go quietly, I don't think I could survive a scene!"

And with that, I lit up the cigarette I been holding and took a long drag— *(She mimes the action)* —and blew the smoke in his face like in a photograph from *The Red Book* and said again: "Just go, I don't think I could survive a scene!"

(A beat.
Lurlene unfreezes from the pose, and slumps.)

REHANA LEW MIRZA

Soldier X

Soldier X *takes us into the heart of the longest war in U.S. history and the particularly heavy repercussions on our young people of color, as they just try to make it through everyday life. The play follows Monica, a uniformed social worker, as she falls for Jay, a recently returned veteran. But Jay falls in love with Amani, the sister of his deceased Muslim comrade, Talib. The tenuous love triangle is tested under the weight of race, religion, and military trauma. This speech takes place in a San Diego dive bar after Monica finds out that Jay has been obsessively pursuing Amani, despite her advice.*

JAY: They said Taliban was hiding out in some housing complex. ROE (rules of engagement) says not to engage
civilians, but in the end, Taliban can be hiding anywhere.
They can be anyone.

And there are these flashes, you know, of light as we
unleash and—they're like, already ghosts. These women
and children, old people—this guy in a wheelchair gets
it, right in the chest, the only part left of him that works.

And fucking Talib. He. I don't even know where he went. I'm just shooting. I can't track everyone.

He— We found him later, bleeding out, covering this little girl. She looked like she could be his sister, just wrapped in his arms, tight. He was just . . . protecting her. When she was already dead.

I don't know, I can't figure out. I can't remember if looking down that scope, maybe I missed him, maybe he came down the side where I couldn't see and I . . . Or maybe I was aiming for that little girl and took him out too. I keep thinking I should know. But the one thing I know? Is that looking at him laid out on the ground, I didn't see my friend. I just saw another dead Muslim. And for all I know I could have pulled the trigger myself.

ANNA MOENCH

Hunger

Hunger *is set in contemporary rural China. Living characters are played by puppets, each manipulated by three puppeteers, manifesting the local belief that each person is animated by three souls. After a character dies, the puppeteers release the puppet and continue as the souls.*

At the start of the play, Xiao Li's mentally ill son, Jian, has committed a school stabbing—the equivalent of a school shooting in a country where guns are unavailable—and takes his own life. In this scene, Xiao Li falls asleep and dreams of the last conversation he had with his son before Jian left home to work as a migrant laborer.

> *(Xiao Li sits on a plastic chair, staring at a small TV. The sounds of a Chinese game show burble out of the TV, tinny and strange. Xiao Li has propped his head on his hand. He drifts off.*
>
> *As he sleeps, Soul 1 sits in the stool next to him.*
>
> *Xiao Li, now an actor, opens his eyes, dreaming. He looks over at Soul 1. He looks back at the TV. They watch together.)*

XIAO LI:

Wanna do karaoke? Or no.
No.

(Silence.)

Used to like karaoke. When you were a kid.
Barely use the damn machine now. Waste of money. I
told you.
Should sell it.
I hate this show.
That girl. Dumb girl. What was her name?
Whatever. Got famous for being on this show.
For saying that thing, what did she say?
You remember.
What was it.

(He thinks, hard. Gives up. Watches TV.
Suddenly:)

"I'd rather cry in a BMW than laugh on the back of a
bicycle." That was it. Famous for that.
Stupid show.

(Watches TV.)

Construction is hard work, Jian. Dangerous. You can't
slack off. Nobody's watching your ass but you.
It's not like out in the fields with me and Ma. Fixing
your fuck-ups. You're expendable. To them. Your boss
doesn't give a fuck. He shouldn't, why should he? He
shouldn't. He won't.
Anyway, don't slack off is what I'm saying.
Look at that. Why are they getting paid to do that, I
mean, what,
who even,
who watches this shit? People get paid to make this
shit because stupid people watch this shit. I can't

believe we're watching this shit.

But.

There's nothing else.

(Watches TV.)

Fuck it, I'm going to bed. You want this on still, or . . .

(Silence. Xiao Li stands up.)

Just don't turn it up too loud.

Hey.

In case I'm gone before you leave.

Don't . . . you gotta keep it together, Jian. You can't
be . . . you can't just . . . nobody will understand
   when you get
into those . . . moods, out there, you know, it's not the
same as being here with people who, who
   understand.

You. And your.

Whatever you wanna call it.

Okay? It's not . . . just . . .

Never mind.

You can't slack off. Is what I'm trying to say.

You'll come home for New Year's, so.

Not too long.

Don't waste your money on alcohol. Nothing but
   trouble
there. Bring that money home. To your mother. Pitch
in, for once. All right?

Night.

*(Xiao Li wakes up, now a puppet. Soul 1 is gone. Xiao Li puts
a hand on the empty chair that Soul 1 has left behind.)*

DOMINIQUE MORISSEAU

Skeleton Crew

This play is about the closing of the last exporting stamping plant in Detroit and a makeshift family of blue-collar workers that help each other through the inevitable news. Reggie (thirties, African American) is a foreman who was once on the blue-collar side. He's now on the ropes, laying off people and struggling to help his co-workers. Here, he tells Faye, a co-worker, that he finally snapped under the pressure and attacked his supervisor after they tried to force him to push her into early retirement.

REGGIE: It was the way he said it that really made me—I just couldn't listen to him talkin' like that. Couldn't let him. Spoke about you like you wasn't even—like you wasn't Faye. Like you had no name or no—history or no—"Dead weight" he say—just like that—like you wasn't even— I just couldn't let him. I felt it in my chest. Like dynamite burstin' inside of me. I attacked him Faye. I fuckin'—I— I attacked him. I attacked my supervisor.

    I'm—I'm done. I just . . . I went for him. Just for a second. Like a shockwave went through me. Lunged at him like I was gonna pound him into the fuckin' ground. Like I was gonna grab him by the collar and crush that shit in my hands. Looked at him in his eyes. Seein' through that emptiness. That lack of feeling. That—whatever you call it—that make you stop seein' yourself in somebody else. And I flexed on him like: "Nigga I wish you would say some shit like that again. I will fuckin' kill you." 'Cept I ain't say it with words. *(Beat)* Then the shockwave left me. Real fast. And I ain't touch him at all. Just got swole on him for a sec. But I came close enough. I would've. And he know it. And I know it too. I see him looking into my eyes like I'm the devil. Can smell his fear. Like if he even breathes louder than a sigh I might kill him dead. And I might've, Faye. I just might've. *(Beat)* And I stand there, froze. Not knowin' if I really reached at him or if it was in my mind. But I see him lookin' at me—stiff. Like I scared the shit outta him. Like he was under attack. Like I'm that nigga. It's nothin' but silence between us for a sec. And then I just say, "NO DEAL." And I walk out.

JULIE MARIE MYATT

Wake Up, Mrs. Moore

Hospital room. Virginia in bed. 1976.

(Alma enters.)

ALMA: It's hot in here. Jesus Christ.

(She tries to open a window.)

I'm sorry I didn't come last week, but Tracy got sick (again) and then Jason was suspended from school so I had to stay home and keep an eye on him all day. Literally. All day. If I don't watch that kid day and night, he will break something, smoke something, or escape. I'm raising a criminal . . . I don't know where I went wrong—well, I didn't go wrong. It's John's fault. He has given his son no guidance whatsoever. If Jason ends up in Folsom Prison finding Jesus and making license plates, he will have his father to thank. I've done nothing but devote my life to that kid. And his little sister. Neither of them show me the slightest bit of appreciation. Thirteen and ten years old, and they talk to me like they're forty-five, drunk, and I'm their whore. Unbelievable, the language. If we had talked to Mother and Dad the way my kids talk to me, we would not have a tooth left in our mouths, I'll tell you that much. I don't know how I put up with it.

(She finally gives up on the window.)

Well, I know how I put up with it. I love them. Obviously. They're the fruit of my loins . . . (Not the best fruit, mind you, but . . . they're still my bananas.) . . . Those two martinis every night before dinner help. Immensely.

(She smiles at Virginia.)

Your hair is just about all grown back, huh? God, we really thought we'd lost you that last time. But, you held on . . . You keep holding on. I tell Glenn, just let her go . . . let you go.

(She takes a brush from her purse and begins to brush Virginia's hair, but brushes her own first.)

Anyway . . . I'm letting my hair grow again. Every time I get a new style, I hate it and John hates it, and we fight because "he's a man that likes long hair so why can't I just do one thing to make him happy," and I have to remind him I do my share of things. To make him happy. Most of which, he does not notice.

(She brushes Virginia's hair.)

I wish I could just be like the Amish or something and stick to one thing . . . To hell with fashion . . . I would think that would be very freeing . . . Although, they spend a lot of time churning butter and making their own clothes and killing pigs and I don't have the patience for all that . . . If I want bacon, I'll go to the store for that, and I'm not going to churn my own butter, for Christ's sake when someone else can make it just as good. Though we've switched to margarine. It's much better for you, and cheaper . . . You wouldn't believe the price of things . . . How does this country celebrate two hundred years? What's our big bicentennial present? Inflation . . . Thank you, Uncle Sam . . . We finally get out of Vietnam, and now we all have to pay for it . . . as if we hadn't paid enough already . . . I think it's what's given Mother cancer . . . And I think Dad is going to drink himself to death one day . . . Sometimes I think they look at me and wonder what happened, where'd all their kids go? . . . One minute they had three, and the next I'm standing at their front door holding a bundt cake, all by myself . . . I catch Mother looking behind me, looking for you and George . . . and then when it's my kids who walk up, she can't hide her disappointment. I get it. I often look at my kids and think, "Where'd these creeps come from?" . . . John is a terrible father . . . Oh, gosh, I almost forgot . . . juicy gossip . . . I had a cup of coffee with my friend Judy before I came over here—you remember Judy . . .

(She stops brushing.)

Of course you do. If you had just waited on her, maybe, maybe, all this would have been different. Maybe. Not that I'm blaming Judy. Or you . . . But . . . it was a few minutes, Virginia. Really. A few minutes. You really are the most impatient person I've ever met . . .

(She resumes brushing.)

Anyway, Judy said she needed to talk. Which is code for my husband is leaving me. Or I'm pregnant. Or so and so tried to kill herself. Or, do you have any pink pills to spare. So, I go over there . . . Turns out, she's having an affair with someone, she wouldn't tell me who, and he won't leave his wife, and she can't leave her husband because she never went to college, and has no skills, and is afraid of landing in the gutter. She and her husband were high-school sweethearts, but she says she really loves this other guy, so she's all wrung out and I ended up giving her one of the pills the dentist gave me when I had that root canal last year as I do find they help most things. (I've had the prescription refilled four times.) I really didn't know what to tell her. I mean, I do have a college degree but what good has it done me? Have I used it? Who really gives a rat's ass about English literature? What's someone going to hire me to do, recite *Beowolf* for three dollars an hour? Save lives with Shakespeare sonnets? Solve world hunger with my paper on Mary Shelley? Yeah, there's about a snowball's chance in hell of that happening. I don't have any more skills than Judy does now . . . It all makes you think . . . Does anyone know what the hell they're doing? . . . Maybe those Amish have it all figured out and we just don't know it . . . You never hear about them getting stuck in affairs, looking for careers, or sticking their head in an oven to end it all.

(Silence.)

Of course they cook with wood.

JANINE NABERS

Annie Bosh Is Missing

Annie Bosh is back. Twenty-two years old and fresh out of rehab, she finds herself working in a bowling alley, living in her mother's ritzy subdivision, and desperate to move on with her life. Slipping out of the front gates, Annie wanders the chaotic streets of a post–Hurricane Katrina Houston, but what exactly is she looking for?

ANNIE: I used to party a lot? I smoked cocaine and heroine together. I did moon rocks . . . That's what they're called. My brother and I used to throw these really wild . . . in Montrose with this best friend I used to have named Kims . . . We had this really crazy night. I got really high and we left. The party. Me and Kims. I can't remember how, but we meet up with these guys and . . . Suddenly we end up back in my dorm? We end up back there and . . . these random guys really want Kims and I to do all this weird stuff? Kims . . . she's, like, totally into it. She wants to fuck me and these guys together, and I. We um . . .

We do it to each other. Kims and I do it but when it comes to hooking up with these guys . . . I can't. I just can't. And Kims. She's too high to care and she *flips out* and they *leave*. They all, like, leave me . . . alone and naked. And I start to *crash*. Because of the drugs, you know? The moon rocks? It's like my whole body has *slammed* into this speeding train and it hurts all over and I can't find more drugs to bring me up again. And I'm naked. And I can't remember what day it is or who I am and I'm like, *fuck it*.

I take one of my coke razors and I . . . .

After. I'm lying on the bathroom tile and I hear this *voice*. I feel this *warm flesh* on my forehead and it's . . . my brother. He, like. Found me. I thought I was dead and he . . .

Have I freaked you out?

Serial Black Face

Atlanta, 1979. The Atlanta child murders grip the entire city. Single mother Vivian copes with the disappearance of her young son while working tirelessly to give a fresh start to her troubled teenage daughter. When a handsome stranger enters her life with promises of new love, she soon learns that nothing is as it seems.

VIVIAN *(In front of a support group)*: It's been 515 days since I last saw my baby. 515 long days.

I go to the police station. I go at least once a week . . . maybe twice. My baby's been gone so long those men down there don't even give me a *second* thought anymore . . . They just pass me by. Like my life doesn't matter. Like my boy doesn't matter.

I keep watching the news . . . every day. *Every* second. I keep seeing coverage of that six-year-old white boy Etan Patz that went missing in Manhattan. And I see his mama on the news . . . and she's crying. And I see all the search parties the police have been leading for him and I see his *face* on my carton of milk . . . and I'm *angry* as hell because fifteen black kids have turned up with their necks cut open . . . and our police ain't doin' shit. And my baby is still nowhere to be found. And I want *answers. We want answers.*

(Other black mothers in the support group cry. They encourage Vivian to continue.)

There are times when I miss my Sammy so much . . . I feel like I'm holding my breath for death . . . Like I'm under water in darkness. And then I remember my husband's face . . . A man who *loves* me. And now . . . I feel . . . I feel like I still have a purpose on this earth . . . Somehow.

MARY KATHRYN NAGLE

Manahatta

Robert explains to his two daughters why he never spoke Lenape in the home, and why he never taught them to speak their own language.

ROBERT: When your mother and I first met, Lenape was all we spoke. I was a kid, about five or six, when the BIA (Bureau of Indian Affairs) showed up.

Walked inside the front door, grabbed me outta my parents' arms, and took me away. My parents didn't speak a word a English. Neither did I, until I got to Riverside. They kept me there for eight years. Made me speak English. Always. Anyone caught speakin' Lenape got a beatin'.

I remember the day I met yer mom. It'd been years since I'd seen my parents, or anyone I knew from home. And your mom, she passed by me in the hall, and she said something. In Lenape. And I, I started to cry. The language. My language. I thought I'd never hear it again. So I responded, in Lenape. But I was too loud. And this teacher, she heard me.

She grabbed my arm real hard and yanked me down the hall, to a closet, where she beat me till I was unconscious. Guess they had to make an example of me, ya know, to make sure none of them other kids started expressin' themselves in Lenape.

My biggest regret is that I didn't speak Lenape with you girls. All these years, I've been ashamed to speak it. Back then, you learned not to speak. Every ounce of your being was spent just tryin' to blend in. Be somethin' you ain't. No matter how much Indian ya had in you, they did their best to whip it out.

One day I woke up and I listened—and then I realized I don't hear it no more. I've lost my wife of sixty years and now that she's gone, ain't no one speakin' it. I buried it. And now it's six feet under.

LYNN NOTTAGE

Sweat

April 2000. A bar.

Tracey (German-American, forties), a hardened steelworker at a metal tubing plant, stands outside of a bar, smoking a cigarette. Her quiet time is interrupted by Oscar (Colombian-American, twenties), the bar's busboy. He produces a flier, which advertises job openings at Tracey's plant. She's insulted by the implication, and becomes upset and nostalgic about her past.

OSCAR: I was born here.

TRACEY: Still . . . you wasn't born here, Berks.

OSCAR: Yeah, I was.

TRACEY: Yeah? Well, my family's been here since the twenties, okay? They built the house that I live in. They built this town. My grandfather was German, and he could build anything. Cabinets, fine furniture, anything. He had these amazing hands. Sturdy. Meaty. Real firm. You couldn't shake his hand without feeling his presence, feeling his power. And those hands, let me tell you, they were solid, worker hands, you know, and they really,

really knew how to make things. Beautiful things. I'm not talking about now, how you got these guys who can patch a hole with spackle and think they're the shit. My grandfather, was the real thing. A craftsman . . . And I remember when I was a kid, I mean eight or nine, we'd go downtown to Penn with Opa. To walk and look in store windows. Downtown was real nice back then. You know, Pomeroy's, Whitner's, whatever. I felt really special, because he was this big, strapping man and people gave him room. But, what I really loved was that he'd take me to office buildings, banks, even the post office . . . you name it, and he'd point out the woodwork that he'd carved. He'd show me the stories that he'd etched into the wood. We could go into any building downtown and somewhere on the woodwork, if you got really, really close he'd point out some detail that he'd carved for me. An apple blossom, honeysuckle, a smiling troll. Really. That's what I'm talking about. It was back when if you worked with your hands people respected you for it. It was a gift. But now, there's nothing on Penn. You go into the buildings, the walls are covered over with sheetrock, the wood painted gray, or some ungodly color, and it just makes me sad. It makes me . . . Whatever.

OSCAR: You okay?

TRACEY: Listen, that piece of paper that you're holding is an insult, it don't mean anything. It'll get you trouble, if you know what I'm saying. Olstead's isn't for you.

JIEHAE PARK

Hannah and the Dread Gazebo

Hannah is a pediatric neurologist. Her grandmother may have committed suicide by jumping off the roof of her retirement home into the Demilitarized Zone between North and South Korea—the governments won't let the family look for the body. Hannah's mother, after what may have been her own suicide attempt, is in the hospital and not waking up.

HANNAH: I met this woman. In the elevator, NYU Medical Center. Thirty-eight, post-doctoral researcher at Columbia, fresh out of the hospital where she had been treated for a Type-3 brain aneurysm that caused a seizure that caused a fall that caused a concussion that caused an MRI that finally, accidentally, caused her doctors to find the benign tumor exerting pressure on her limbic system that had caused the deep deep depression that had always made her think there was something wrong with her head, caused her to exclaim on rainy days that there was something wrong with her head she was so unhappy this wasn't normal there must be something wrong with her head, causing her mother and father to send her to sympathethic-eyed psychiatrists who prescribed Prozac and Zoloft and a long list of hard-to-pronounce SSRIs [selective serotonin re-uptake inhibitors] that caused her despair for not fixing the pounding feeling that something was wrong wrong wrong with her head head head until finally she gave up and decided to fuck it just live with the pounding the pounding that must be the way that everyone felt they just never talked about it at least she had five fingers on each hand and five toes on each foot and the sun in the morning and the moon at night.

So yeah, they found this tumor. And she was healed.

peerless

After some really dark times, D had a vision that led him to take a self-actualization course, lose thirty pounds, and get into a prestigious college. Now he is at the school dance with the girl of his dreams and her twin sister (who unbeknownst to him, are plotting his murder).

D: I once licked a cashew and it sent me to the hospital for three days. Just licked it, you know? Didn't even put the whole thing in my mouth.

And my face got all puffy, like—

Last week I picked up a walnut with both pinkies just to see what would happen and I didn't die but my hands puffed up. I still can't bend my pinky-knuckles.

My counselor says that's why no matter how much weight I lose I'm still fat in my head—I mean why I think I'm fat in my head, because there's some sort of unconscious-association going on with food and death and also maybe that's why I use food to address anxiety, because there's this unconscious association with food and death and I've got an unconscious death wish.

I'm talking a lot
I talk a lot
My mom (says)
This isn't interesting
For other people
It makes them think I'm fragile
I'm not fragile
Or maybe
I was fragile
But now I have NO FEAR
I GO
I DO
I GO
I'm going to stop talking now.

LISA RAMIREZ

To the Bone

Written in the tradition of John Steinbeck's Of Mice and Men, To the Bone *is a contemporary two-act drama that gives the audience a close-up look into the lives of the invisible workforce, those who put food on our table. The play examines the very nature of equality and justice in contemporary America through the eyes of five Central American women whose migration to the U.S. in search of a better life brings its own test of the human spirit. In the scene below, Juana tells Carmen, the story of her missing daughter.*

JUANA: I see you like the sleeping bag. *(Slight pause)* I'm so glad. *(Slight pause)* I bought it for my daughter— *(Slight pause)* —and now you're using it. And I'm happy about that.

(Pause.)

I came here. I came here first. With nothing—like most of us. I worked. I saved money. I worked. I worked until I had enough money to pay—to pay for her crossing. They told me it would cost more for a child. For six thousand dollars her safety and protection were guaranteed. *(Slight pause)* Do you know how long it takes to save six thousand dollars here? How many chickens I had to cut for that?

(She laughs a little.)

We had a plan. I was to wire the money to the Western Union in Guatemala. They'd be by her side from start to finish. They had done this before. She was to carry my address and phone number in two different plastic bags. She was to travel light. Clothes with pockets were best. *(Slight pause)* They gave me the number to their cell phone. I called it. It was good. She would call me as soon as she was leaving my mother's house. She did. I called the cell phone again just to make sure. It was good. *(Slight pause)* We had a plan. She would call me from the river before they crossed into Mexico. She did. She would call me when she got to Mexico. She did. They were to spend the night there and continue on through Mexico the next day. She would call me before they left. She did. She told me she would be traveling with a group of eleven and a half—seven children, four adults, and one baby. She thought it was funny to call the baby "half." I told her that I remembered when she was a "half." And we laughed. *(Slight pause)* She would call me when she arrived at the next border. And she didn't. I called the cell phone. No answer. I called my mother. No word. I called the cell phone again. Disconnected.

(Pause.)

And now—I'm waiting. And praying. *(Slight pause)* And the days—they feel like years. *(Slight pause)* But—I have not given up. I have not given up hope. Nor should you. *(Slight pause)* I bought this for my daughter. And now you're using it, Carmen! And I'm glad.

THERESA REBECK

Zealot

The British Consulate, in Mecca, the first day of the hajj. An American diplomat informs the British consul that she has heard through channels that "something might happen," and then it does. A group of women remove their headscarves within the mosque and start a stampede. One of these women arrives at the consulate, seeking sanctuary. She claims she was doing what Allah told her to do. The local government intend to arrest her as an infidel. Is she a provocateur, or is she Joan of Arc?

EDGAR *(Snapping)*: Yes we could have another fascinating digression into the laws of God versus the laws of man but unless some giant, winged creature with a flaming sword were suddenly to appear in our midst and explain that this really really is what the big guy wants, no one is going to give a shit! God is not even as real as television to any of these people, they are more afraid of television, truth be told, and yes I am going to just say it, you are a woman, so no one cares what you say, even if God himself told you to say it. Women are supposed to keep their mouths shut, and did I mention, no one believes in God? All anyone believes in is blood and oil.

Blood and oil. Is in fact what our governments believe in. And while we may not participate in some of the traditions which different Islamic cultures embrace, we have taken a sworn oath not to interfere in the internal workings of said traditions. The only time it becomes our business is when something or someone threatens to disrupt the flow of oil to our own people, who are living their lives according to their own traditions, far across the sea. And when something happens to that flow of oil because someone decided to interfere in somebody else's oh so clever traditions, wars start, a lot of blood is spilt, and that's the sort of thing that people care about as well. And I'm not talking about a few people, I'm talking about a lot, a very large number of people get upset. Our job, yours and mine, is to keep things from getting to that point. You recall this, yes?

GABRIELLE REISMAN

Catch the Wall

After a New Orleans bouncer MC dies, middle-schoolers Cleo and Justice plot a music video so that their mentor's memory can live on. As the MC's ghost tangles with the girls' Teach for America teachers, students and educators push back against a button-down charter school climate, and work to get their own stories heard.

After being suspended for pushing a young teacher, thirteen-year-old Justice describes a day at her new alternate school on the fringes of the Orleans Parish School District.

JUSTICE: It take me two hours to get to Schwartz. Gotta get up at 5:30 just to wait for that bus. That bus go all over the whole city. Pickin' up no one.

The first day at Schwartz, I had been the only one in the classroom.

Teacher didn't even talk to me. She just read on her iPad and I straight just sat. And waited. An' waited.

I was like, "Miss. Miss! I don't have my assignment."

She just looked up, then went back to her game or whatever.

For seven hours.

The second day, I could go to lunch. But they got the nastiest lunches in there. Like mealworms in the cream corn. An' red beans that smelled straight like feet. And they had mice.

Not like a few, like all the schools had. They got like a nest of mice in the bathroom and a girl in ninth grade said they got a whole pack a rats runnin' 'round in the boiler room, so nobody even goes down there. That's why there's no hot water . . .

No one can talk in the hall. Or at lunch. Or at all.

Everyone's afraid of each other. Everyone got beef with each other 'cause half of them kids got sent there for fighting with each other.

The third day, I had my Love hoodie on.

They have like these interventionists. These *big* men who stand up in the hallway, with bats.

Interventionist said take my Love hoodie off.

I said I was cold. He said I didn't ask you if you was comfortable. I said I was cold and he picked me up by the base of my neck and he slammed me, into the floor. Held me there by my hair. With my cheek in the lunch mess.

Everybody cheesing.

I didn't go to school today.

AMELIA ROPER

Lottie in the Late Afternoon

A comedy. End of Act I. Saturday afternoon. A small New England vacation house on the edge of a terrifying cliff. Four awkward people disappoint each other and themselves. Lottie is sitting on the porch in the sun with a huge pile of books she will never read. Her best friend, Clara, is in love with Anne, who has just had a painful abortion, and her husband, Ryan, can't access his antianxiety app without the internet. Lottie and Clara are alone. Lottie pretends to read A Passage to India. *Clara has meat in a plastic bag.*

Slashes indicate overlapping dialogue.

LOTTIE: So here we are.

CLARA: Here we are.

LOTTIE: In this beautiful house, you're not even paying for it.

CLARA: Thanks.

LOTTIE: We thought about asking you but we didn't.

CLARA: Thanks?

LOTTIE: You even get the room with the afternoon sun! And you're miserable.

CLARA: I'm not miserable.

LOTTIE: You're miserable without Anne and you're making me miserable.

CLARA: I'm walking into town.

LOTTIE: You can't.

CLARA: Why?

LOTTIE: Because you just came from town!

CLARA: So?

LOTTIE: And you have meat.

(Clara takes the meat inside. She returns with wine.)

Did you put the meat / in the fridge?

CLARA: / Yes I put the meat in the fridge!

(They drink.)

LOTTIE: Yesterday, as we were driving here, when we were close to the town I was thinking, please be beautiful, please be a beautiful town! Please have, colored, hand-painted signs and flags and please let each shop be a different brick and let there be at least one tree I like and things I want to buy in the shops, or not buy but pick up and touch. Let me meet someone nice, in funny clothes, someone old maybe who smiles.

CLARA: Well there's a boutique electronics store. Aside from that, it's pretty. Yeah, it is very pretty actually. I like it. Good choice.

LOTTIE: I'm glad you think so.

CLARA: You don't think so?

LOTTIE: I haven't seen it yet! We didn't drive through it yesterday, we went around.

I thought the locals would be, I don't know, doing their banking and it would be faster to go around. We had meat, so.

CLARA: We can go back after dinner.

LOTTIE: It doesn't matter.

CLARA: Let's go after dinner.

LOTTIE *(Smiles)*: Okay, thanks.
  What did you buy?

CLARA: Lamb. Anne chose lamb. She wanted beef but when she saw it in the window she changed her mind.

LOTTIE: Oh dear! Because of all the blood,

CLARA: Because it was too expensive. Really. The beef is more expensive because of the flooding, the guy said, which is weird to me because lambs are shorter—

LOTTIE: Lambs float.

CLARA: What?

LOTTIE: They float until they can, land again, like a balloon.

CLARA: No they don't.

LOTTIE: Well I don't know. It's really very freeing, not having any internet, we can just say things.

(They smile. They drink.)

CLARA: I've missed you.

LOTTIE: I miss you too.

CLARA: Wait. Have I? No, I haven't missed you, just then though, in that moment, that was a nice moment, and I thought, what a surprise, when was the last one?

LOTTIE: Clara.

CLARA: Are you jealous because I'm Anne's friend or her lover I wonder.

LOTTIE: Friend.

CLARA: Hmm.

LOTTIE: I only kissed you once, because I really liked your outfit and I got confused. I only kissed you once and we were twelve.

CLARA: Twenty-two.

LOTTIE: You had the best clothes! But you are still my best friend and I think about you all the time.

CLARA: No you fucking don't.

LOTTIE: I, how are your, mom and dad?

CLARA: Lottie.

LOTTIE: What? Did they die?

CLARA: No they're fine.

LOTTIE: Are they still in the same house?

CLARA: Yeah.

LOTTIE: Do they still have the cat?

CLARA: Oh, not that house. No, they're in, they moved. And that cat died. That's not why they moved.

LOTTIE: Tell them I said hi.

CLARA: They won't remember who you are.

LOTTIE: Oh.

CLARA: Call me more.

LOTTIE: I—

CLARA: No. You don't.

LOTTIE: But I invited you here. It's a new thing I'm trying, and I am trying.

CLARA: Thank you for inviting me.

LOTTIE: Thank you for coming. I'm sorry about the cliff! There was no mention of cliff on the website, there was no picture.

CLARA: It's fine. The house is pretty, the sea is pretty.

LOTTIE: The house and the sea! Not the cliff in between the house and the sea! It said short walk! What does that mean for a cliff? Short walk?

CLARA: The steps,

LOTTIE: I saw the steps.

CLARA: So it's fine!

LOTTIE: I don't want this weekend to be fine! I want it to be great! I want it to be—

CLARA: It will be, great! The steps are, inconvenient.

LOTTIE: You have to go all the way around.

CLARA: The sea is pretty.

LOTTIE: But to get to it, to get to it, oh listen to us, the sea, the sea, the inconvenience! Some people can't afford vacations. Some people are dead!

(Lottie chugs her wine, all her wine.)

I think being a teenager in the eighties is a huge disadvantage, our nostalgia is fluorescent, nothing will ever be that bright again. Don't laugh at me.

MELISSA ROSS

Of Good Stock

Jess, Amy, and Celia Stockton are the last living members of their family, and the heirs to their deceased novelist father's legacy. They gather for a weekend at the family's home in Cape Cod to celebrate oldest sister Jess's birthday, her first in the midst of her treatment for breast cancer. And more importantly, symbolically passing the age their mother lost her own battle with the disease when they were children. After a night of family bickering and chaos leads to the sudden and unexplained departure of her fiancé, Amy retreats to the dock behind the house.

Slashes indicate overlapping dialogue.

(11:11 P.M.

Amy sits at the edge of the dock finishing up a call and a cry. Jess stands a bit away, holding two glasses of scotch.)

AMY: Uh-huh. Yeah okay. *(She looks up—sees Jess—and then looks back away)* Okay. Okay. *(Beat)* Okay. *(She hangs up)* Whadya know. 11:11.

JESS: Was / that Josh.

AMY: Make a wish.

JESS: Is / he okay?

AMY: Make a wish! *(Pause)* You got one?

JESS: Yup.

(They both close their eyes and wish. Eyes open. Beat.)

Was that Josh?

AMY: I thought I told you not. To follow me?

JESS: Is / he all right?

AMY: Didn't I? Didn't I ask that?

JESS: Maybe? I uh. *(Beat)* Brought you a scotch? *(No response)* I figure whether you want company or not, you won't turn down a glass of Dad's forty-year / -old scotch.

AMY: What do you want.

JESS: Just making sure / you're okay.

AMY: I'm okay!

JESS: Are you / sure?

AMY: *Yes. (Beat)* Sorry for. Ruining your party.

JESS: You didn't *ruin* anything. We. *(Beat)* We were all being insensitive.

AMY: Oh that's okay I'm. Used to it by now. *(Beat)* You can't fix this.

JESS: I'm not trying to.

AMY: Sure you are. Ever since we were kids you. Follow. Me and Cee around like we're your. *Ducklings.*

JESS: I / do not.

AMY: No matter how many times we try to run away from you. We can't get too far. You're always *right there*. Fixing. Doting. Smothering. Your poor little. Motherless sisters. *(She holds out a hand for the scotch)* One of those is mine?

(Jess hands her a glass. Amy takes it.)

Thanks.

(Silence. They drink.)

JESS: Can I come sit?

AMY *(Shrugs)*: It's your house. You can. Do whatever you want.

(Jess sits next to her. They dunk their feet in the water. They sip their scotch.)

JESS: We should have a boat.

AMY: *You* can / get a boat.

JESS: We have a *dock*. We should / have a *boat*.

AMY: What we *should* do is sell it.

JESS: The dock?

AMY: The dock the house the / whole thing.

JESS: I can't do that.

AMY: Fine whatever / Jess fine.

JESS: I love this house.

AMY: Ugh. I *hate* this house.

JESS: How could you hate / this house???

AMY: All I see everywhere I look is *Diane*.

JESS: Ugh Diane??? / Ugh. Why.

AMY: It's all her *stuff*. All her awful bland mediocre Midwestern / stuff.

JESS: It's not so bad.

AMY: It's not us! She threw out everything that reminded her of Mom—including some things that were really special to me.

JESS: Like what.

AMY: It doesn't matter *what*. *Specifically*. It's all. Gone. *(Beat)* She wasn't nice. She didn't want us around. *(Beat) You* don't know. *You* were in college. *You* never came home. But. For me and Cee? The three summers we had a stepmother were really. Horrifying. *(Beat)* I ran into her at a Pilates class in Soho. She had a really bad face-lift. *(They both laugh)* We should sell the house and let somebody make a movie out of one of the books.

JESS: I will be doing neither / of those things.

AMY: Come on! Those books are our legacy! And we're not *doing* anything / with them.

JESS: I'm not selling the rights to the books!

AMY: Fine! Then sell the house!

JESS: No! / Absolutely not!

AMY: It's a pain in the ass and far away. And whenever we're here it's a disaster.

JESS: Believe it or not? I actually *like* seeing you.

AMY: If that were *really* true Jess? We both know we'd see each other more often when we. Live in the same city.

JESS: *(Beat)* I love you Ame. You / know that.

AMY: I know. *(A laugh)* In your own way. *(She finishes off her scotch)* You should've brought the bottle.

(Pause.)

JESS: Our *parents* are. In that ocean.

AMY: Their *ashes* are in that ocean.

JESS: I can't sell the house when they are both / out there!

AMY: Good god. He's been dead for almost ten years and you *still* need to be the favorite!

JESS: I do not!

AMY: Sure you do! So wherever he is he can see sweet obedient Jess doing *exactly* what he wanted till the day she *died*, right? You win!

JESS: I don't *want* / to *win*.

AMY: Took care of his house. Check. Babied his books? Check. Married the guy he handpicked / for you.

JESS *(Laughing)*: He did not / handpick Fred.

AMY: When're you gonna live your life for *you*? *(Pause)* Fuck. Some day *I'm* gonna be dead and. Also in that ocean probably and. What will be *my* legacy? Huh? Being the *daughter* of somebody who did something great?

JESS: It's okay to be just a regular person you know.

AMY *(Laughs)*: Yeah well. I can't even manage *that*. My father won a Pulitzer Prize. I can't even seem to. Procreate. *(She points to her stomach and whispers)* Apparently I've got *rotten eggs*.

JESS: Aw Ame / I'm sorry.

AMY: What does it matter anyway. Looks like I don't have a baby daddy anymore so. Que sera fucking sera.

(Pause.)

JESS: *I* wasn't the favorite. *Cee's* the favorite.

AMY: No it was you. It was close. But it was you. *(Beat)* I think he just *liked* you best. As a *person*.

JESS: Well you were *Mom's* favorite.

AMY: Who knows. I barely remember her.

JESS: You *were*. I used to get so. *Jealous*. The way you'd always cuddle up in bed with her and talk and talk. Like old friends. *(Beat)* You look just like her.

AMY: I know.

JESS: You're like her twin.

AMY: *(Beat)* Yeah well. I guess that's *my* legacy, huh? I get to look like my. Beautiful. Dead mom.

SHARYN ROTHSTEIN

All the Days

All the Days *is a family dramedy about Ruth Zweigman, sixties, a retired bank teller and force of nature, who comes to stay with her daughter, Miranda, thirties, and worn-out, for the two weeks before Miranda's son's bar mitzvah. Ruth and Miranda have always had a tense relationship, but her son's bar mitzvah, as well as the recent death of Miranda's brother, have forced mom and daughter into the same two-bedroom apartment and back into each other's lives. This monologue takes place the night before Jared's bar mitzvah. Miranda has just found her son with a backpack on, trying to sneak out to his dad's house. Ruth intervenes just after her daughter and grandson have blown up at each other. Ruth speaks to Jared, but Miranda is there too, listening.*

RUTH: You know your mother was always threatening to run away. I always thought she was full of it, but then one time we had a big fight, all about whether her hair was too long—it was—and I went to her room and she was gone. I think she was a couple years older than you are now. Just gone. Not even a note.

The police were no help, thought she had a boyfriend. Her friends hadn't seen her. This was before cell phones of course. So finally, out of my mind, I drive over to Grandpa's. There she was, sitting outside his apartment building, right off the Expressway in the middle of Queens. Apparently he wasn't home. He told her he would be, but he wasn't. She'd been there for hours. I picked her up and we went—you remember? For pancakes. Giant stacks of pancakes. Every kind they had on the menu. She had to feed all that hair.

So she worries. You want to spend the night with your dad, a big night like this, she worries you're gonna be let down somehow. She worries she's not going to be able to protect you. That when you come back to her, you'll be hurt, and you'll think maybe the hurt is somehow her fault . . . To you it seems like one night. But when you're a mom, there's never enough nights, never enough days with your kid . . . to miss even one . . .

So. How'd I do? You feel guilty enough to stay?

TANYA SARACHO

Fade

Mexican-born Lucia is a first-time TV writer on a cutthroat TV show. She soon discovers that the Chicano studio custodian, Abel, has a windfall of plot ideas. As their friendship grows, his stories start to blur with hers—with unexpected consequences.

ABEL: No, pos my wife, um, ex-wife, she's from El Salvador. She didn't have papers when I met her. But I fell for her hard so then I didn't care about that shit. I was all empelotado so we did everything real fast . . . the wedding, todo shotgun. And like six months later Melita came. That's my baby girl's name, Melanie, but we call her Melita. But like with all of these situations, I'm convinced it was doomed from the start. My ex is real jealous and very passionate. Who knew that Central Americans were so feisty? I always thought they were the calm ones. Anyway, I didn't know she would turn out to be a liona. She was on her best behavior right up until we moved into our own place in Boyle Heights. For like around six months everything was good. Pretty nice actually. And then, I don't know what happened but she started—truth be told is I think she was sniffing, but I still can't prove that. She had this aunt that came to live with us and she would always start drama with us. And the thing is, it was like affecting the baby. She'd leave with her aunt God-knows-where and I'd come home and the baby would be all alone, crying in the crib. But if I would say anything, the both of them would pounce on me. Para no hacertela larga we split up and then it got, just, it got bad. La tia, she came to my job, not here, I used to be a fireman, actually, so she came to the firehouse y armo un desmadre saying that "this and that," that now that my wife had her citizenship she was going to take the baby back to El Salvador and not tell me where. And like other shit. They were also taking money from my account and wouldn't tell me for what. Just shady shit. I don't know what the two of them were into, who even knows if that lady was even her aunt, you know? I think about that now. Was she even her tia? Anyway, one day la tia comes to my work and says that they're leaving that day. —So I run over there and all her cousins—well, that's who she says they are, but I never met no cousins of her's before—they're like six of them in the front yard. And something didn't look right. The whole thing . . . God, I've played it back in my mind, over and over. Drove me nuts while I was locked up. Something just wasn't right that day. Anyway, I go in and my ex is like half dressed and all wyled out. Sweaty and hyper. The baby crying on the floor there with like two big Salvatrucha-looking dudes. But who knows right? Could have been her cousins but I don't know. I didn't want to find out. I just wanted my baby. So I start telling Silvia—that was my ex's name—I tell her that she can't take my baby. That I won't let her take her. And let me tell you, hell really hath no fury. This bitch, she's about this big but she can get crazy. Throwing shit, spitting out things you wouldn't even write on a bathroom wall. The MS dudes give us some space I guess because they go outside. And I grab Melita and try to get her diaper bag to just take her away while Silvia calms down. But as soon as I do that, the fucking tia comes out of nowhere and starts beating me with the fucking curling iron and then Silvia just goes nuts and grabs a knife. And she starts waving that thing around. So I'm trying to make my way out the door, but I got the aunt beating me and then Silvia slashing at me. Cutting deep too. And then she stabs me. Like for real. And I say to her, "I got the baby in my arms you fucking maniac! What the fuck is wrong with you?!" No consideration for the baby in my arms. What if she stabbed her? But that bitch won't listen cuz she's like an animal. And when she's about to lunge at me again I just punch her right on the nose. I just floored her. Blood squirting everywhere. Then, the tia comes at me and I roundhouse that fucking bitch too. Nobody's caring about Melita—these fucking bitches. My poor baby in my arms, hysterical. Imagine having to see that? That baby is my whole world. I don't give a fuck if it's her mother, I won't let nobody hurt her. I tried walking out but that didn't work so good. I got attacked by all them cousins—me, with my daughter in my arms. Pinches culeros. The cops came and of course, Silvia turned it into me being an abuser and well . . . I'm the one that got locked up.

(Pause.)

It's fine. I got my daughter with me now, which is all that matters.

The Tenth Muse

It's 1715, in the Convent of San Jeronimo, Colonial New Spain, in what became the capital city of Mexico—twenty years after the death of the feminist nun Sor Juana Inés de la Cruz. The same convent where Sor Juana lived and died. San Jeronimo was once a religious residency for rich girls of Spanish descent whose families could afford the dowry and upkeep; each nun got up to three servants. Tomasita, a young Mexica slave, is one of these servants.

TOMASITA: Sometimes I imagine I am a great big eagle. I swoop down and take animals, take snakes in my beak. Tear their flesh as easy as if it was nixtamal. I dream that dream sometimes.

(Beat.)

I asked my Tata what this dream meant, because he has the gift of knowing these things and he told me I should not dream it because it was a warrior's dream. A man's dream. So when it comes in the night, the vision of me as an eagle soaring, I try to jump out of my sleep, and dream of just the darkness. Because I think there is no harm in dreaming of a blackness.

LAURA SCHELLHARDT

The Comparables

In The Comparables *three women vie for power in the cutthroat world of high-end reality. Bette runs her own female-dominated agency. Monica is her loyal second-in-command. Iris is the savvy new hire. When Bette's reputation falls under attack, the future of the agency is at stake. Who, if anyone, will survive the ordeal, and to what lengths will they go to ensure success? The play is a dark comedy that begs the question: For women in the competitive world, is there more than one way to do business? Bette delivers this speech to the members of the Association for Women Entrepreneurs, at the onset of her professional ordeal, when she's just beginning to suspect her reputation is in jeopardy.*

BETTE: When I was twenty-five I landed a position at a high-profile agency. I was their *only* female agent, which might be surprising today, but back then it was not exceptional. *I* was exceptional, the situation was not.

   And I endured the hassle one might expect—missed invitations, snickering in the corridor, the sticky looks up and down—and in spite of it all, I made my first six-figure sale. And the day after closing I was given a party and a cake, and during this party the head broker pulled me aside, and he apologized if there'd been ill will amongst *the boys*—and here's something I've learned, folks, whenever grown men are referred to as *the boys*, something asinine is about to occur.

But I said I bore no grudge, and he replied, "You're a smart girl, *you know your place.*" And he excused himself and went to the bathroom to take a piss, and I know that because he left the door open. So I could watch.

Naturally, I reported this to management, and they sent a woman to take my statement, and do you know what she advised? She said, *"Darling,* I find it's better if you keep your head down. After all, no one promised us a walk in the park."

And I ask you now, as I asked myself then: Who is worse in this scenario—him or her? Both are bad, but who, in your minds, is worse? . . .

I listened to her though, I kept my head down. Then some months later, there was a convention out of town, and I was handed an itinerary from one of *the boys* saying our flight left at one P.M. the next day. It wasn't until I got to the airport that I learned the flight did not exist, and my colleagues had departed hours before. I quit that day, and I've never looked back.

I don't say this out of anger, nor is it a cautionary tale. I say it because this is what I know: If you want to be successful as a woman in this world—keep your head *up*, get rid of *the boys*, and for god's sake, learn to fly your own plane.

HEIDI SCHRECK

The Consultant

Barbara (forty–sixty) used to work at a pharmaceutical advertising company called Sutton, Feingold and McGrath. Then, she discovered a cult-like corporate self-help group that taught her to maximize her deepest human potential, and it transformed her life. In this scene, Barbara returns to her old company to try to convert a young secretary stuck in its suffocating environment.

BARBARA:
    Your life can be
    Whatever you imagine it can be
    But you have to imagine it first . . .
    I didn't know that while I was working here
    I couldn't see it

    This place is sick it's not bad it's not evil
    But it is sick and it's not your fault you can't see it
    You're buried deep inside
    The Organism
    But think about it

In a hundred years, will this building even be here
This building will probably be razed to the ground
And your grandchildren
If they tell stories about you
They won't be stories about how you
Worked as a secretary in a pharmaceutical advertising
    company
I mean let's face it even if you work your way up
Become an account manager
Do you want to work your way up
No?
You girls!
You're aiming too low
What happened?
There was a moment, when I was in my twenties
There was this golden moment
And I'm not saying you girls you frittered it away
It's not your fault I don't blame you
In fact in many ways I take responsibility
My generation I mean should take responsibility
My daughter I bought her the album *Free to Be You and
    Me*
Do you remember this album:
"Every boy in this land grows to be his own man
In this land every girl grows to be her own woman"
My daughter wore that record out
I had to buy her a new copy
My daughter
She's a teacher now, which is a very honorable
    profession obviously
But not what we were fighting for in the seventies
The opportunity for women to become teachers was not
Our goal
That would be like fighting for women to become
    nurses or
Actresses or something

(Barbara smiles.)

The thing that happens to us Amelia
Is that we get stuck with the story we tell ourselves
It's not so much that the past haunts us
Or that we're carrying it around like a snail carries
His house on his back
It's that we make The Past Our Future
Like you with all your student loans
You see?
That's your future

(Beat.)

What are you doing tonight
I'm going to this seminar
No pressure
But
Since I started attending these courses
I've quit my job and started my own business
I make thirty percent more money than I was making
Here and I was making good money
Here
I don't have to deal with Harold anymore
I'm dressing better
I know what colors look good on me
I've found a new apartment that is
Just
It's filled with light
It's near Prospect Park
I go for an hour-long walk every day
I can do that because you see I make
My own schedule
I make my own life
Does that sound like something that
Would interest you? . . .

Grand Concourse

Shelley is a forty-year-old Catholic nun who works in a Bronx soup kitchen. She recently hired a new employee, a nineteen-year-old girl named Emma, who idolizes her. In this scene, Emma wants to know how Shelley decided to become a nun: Did she have a vision? Emma: "I always thought God came to people in the night and said, 'Come with me.'" Shelley confesses that she did indeed have a kind of vision, but it was not as exciting as Emma's fantasy.

Note: Shelley dresses in regular work clothes, not a traditional nun's habit.

SHELLEY:

It was technically more of a dream than a vision
I had this dream about a boy in my school
. . . Rob Kolker.

(Shelley looks at Emma.)

Yeah it was not like that okay
Rob was a junior when I was a freshman
Everyone had a crush on him he wore a cowboy hat
and later he ended up living on a sailboat
Anyway
In the dream I was wearing a dress
I was wearing the dress I wore to my high school prom
    and
I used to have horrible eczema in high school
And in this dream my eczema was out of control
it manifested as these
huge weeping sores and I
I was awash in shame
I felt like an affront to humanity
like how dare I go around offending the world with
    my . . .
with all of this.

(Shelley gestures to her whole self.)

So in the dream I was curled up in Rob Kolker's lap
and he was looking down at me at my weeping sores
        and
I wanted to die
I wanted to die
I knew that he must be looking at me with
contempt or disgust or
I was waiting to be annihilated by his disgust
but instead he said . . .

(Beat.)

He said:
. . . You are adorable.

(Long beat.)

And he was looking down at me with such gentleness
that I understood I was
received
in my entirety
weeping sores and all
that my body was not an affront but a
I'm sorry I know this sounds dorky but
I don't have any other words
I understood that my body was holy
that I am holy
and when I woke up I knew that it was possible
to look at myself like this
and at others
with gentleness with
Adoration.

(Beat.)

Yeah it's hard to . . .
It loses something in the speaking.

JENNY SCHWARTZ

Somewhere Fun

Present day. Rosemary Rappaport, late fifties, is talking to her old friend, Cecelia. They are lunching at a restaurant on Manhattan's Upper East Side.

ROSEMARY: I'll always have a rare sort of bond, as they say, with Evelyn Armstrong; as well as baby Beatrice, who was, quite simply, the most beautiful living being you ever did see, to behold as well as, inside and out, divine; didn't whine, didn't cry, never had a single, excuse the expression, accident; I know, I know what you're thinking, all little children have accidents, and that's perfectly fine, to be expected, from time to time, and possibly even encouraged, maybe they're acting out, maybe they haven't learned to control their itsy-bitsy, teensy-weensy bladders; I don't know, I'm not what you'd call an expert on child-rearing, for that matter.

I've said enough.

But Beatrice Armstrong emerged from the womb with expert bladder control, not to mention a considerably high tolerance for pain, because whenever she took a spill, skinned a knee, stubbed a toe, she'd carry on laughing, like a little piece of music, smiling away, an angel from up above. Now, I don't mean to suggest she was a priss or a prig, because by no means, in fact she loved to horse around with boys as well as girls, a real winner she was, perfect teeth, button nose, rosebud mouth, steady boyfriend, varsity everything, student government, honor roll, Model United Nations, never went through one of those awkward stages, gawky stages, even though she was terrifically long-limbed, like some kind of otherworldly, suffice it to say, she was always very comfortable in her skin.

And then she went away to college, and everything sort of fell apart; poor thing wouldn't come out of her room, etcetera, etcetera, refused to eat, refused to bathe, flunking all her subjects, skinnier and skinnier, limbs getting longer and longer, and then finally, Evelyn and T, he's called T, just the letter, short for Townsend if memory serves, they yank her out of school, and they all go, I quote, to intense family therapy—intense.

And it turned out, the problem was, Beatrice Armstrong had always wanted a dog. And why wouldn't her parents get her a dog? What do you want for Christmas? A dog. What do you want for your birthday? A dog. Year after year after year after year. A dog a dog a dog a dog. And why wouldn't her parents go ahead and get her one?

She'd clearly proved herself responsible, deserved to be rewarded, no allergies to speak of, and so what about shedding? Haven't you ever heard of a vacuum cleaner? A Dustbuster? You couldn't pick a lint roller out of a lineup, Evelyn Armstrong, overlooking Central Park; you and your countless country clubs; your charitable causes; I hope your stupid summer home slides smack into the sea; art collection and all. I don't know. Not being a dog lover. I happen to be a cat person myself.

And so they did, Evelyn and T, got her a dog, a Dalmation, and very quickly they discovered he was deaf, which is actually very common for the breed.

Now, Evelyn and T wanted to return him to the breeder, but Beatrice said, no, we love each other for our flaws, is what she said, or something to that effect, and how can you argue with an angel, and so they kept him.

And then, something happened, and I don't know all the details, but Beatrice Armstrong must have approached him from behind, the Dalmation, and deaf as he was, he didn't hear her coming, and unfortunately, but not out of malice, the dog goes and bites off her face. The whole kit and caboodle, in one fell swoop, I'm afraid so.

But this was a while back. This was a while back now. Must be almost a decade, no, must be over a decade the poor thing's been without—

JEN SILVERMAN

The Hunters

Alex and Cameron are Vietnamese-American brothers who, despite their shared career as male hustlers, are going in very different directions. Alex is focused on his desire to get ahead, while Cam is obsessed with family history, in which their Vietnamese grandfather was shot in the back by an American soldier named Marcus Hunter. Cam believes that the ripple effect from this act of violence is responsible for the poverty and disempowerment in which he and his brother are living. The play begins right after Cam has tracked down and kidnapped Marcus Hunter's grandson, a well-to-do New England blue blood named Lyman. As the play unfolds, both brothers must confront the thin line between reparations and revenge, and ask: For how many generations do we carry the weight of past wrongs? Should we—or can we—ever put that weight down?

In this monologue, Lyman Hunter lies unconscious in the bathtub, while Cam explains to Alex how he found him.

CAM: I found him piece by piece. His name, his work, his address, his gym. I thought: I just want to see where he lives. Just want to see the car, the lawn, the well-behaved dog. Just need to see it.

So I looked through his windows, I saw all his books, his leather couches. Couldn't stop thinking about him.

Took four times before we talked. I'd have a cigarette outside his gym, he'd come out and get in his car and drive away. And he didn't see me! He looked straight through me. He didn't think he needed to know who I was. And then one day I offered him a light. By then I knew the cigarettes he liked, the books he liked, the drinks he liked. He was someone who liked attention, and I knew that too. So we started talking.

I had another play in mind, but when I saw the way he looked at me, I thought of what *you* always say, Alex: *Use what you have.* So I did. And we traded numbers, we traded texts. I'd be with a client and Lyman would be texting: *What's up, what're you doing.* And then one night he invited me to a fancy hotel bar. Just a place he liked to go after work, he said. And he bought me drink after drink.

I didn't know what I was going to do. After all that time, can you imagine? I sat at that bar with him and I didn't know what I was going to do. I just knew I had to . . . sit across from him. Smell him. I had to see: what it looks like, how it's built. Him and his father and his grandfather. How three generations walk under one skin. How that beautiful animal moves.

I always thought I'd hate him, sort of right away? But then once he was real—and he was nervous, trying to impress me—then I had to see if I could still hate him.

I slept with him that night. He asked me to come up to his room and I think he thought I'd say no, and then I said yes. And I didn't know yet if I could hate him. So I slept with him again, and then again.

And some time passed. Because I didn't know.

And sometimes it felt— We'd be at a restaurant and he'd tell a joke, or, he'd be driving and he'd lean over and kiss me and . . . It felt—right then—so . . . normal. Like I could almost forget all the things I knew. Like maybe

I didn't even want to know them. And then I hated *myself* for that. But I still didn't know if I could hate *him*.

And then this morning, he was getting dressed. I was in bed and I looked at him putting on his nice shirt and his nice tie and his nice shoes, about to drive back to Connecticut and have lunch with his nice fiancée and her nice family. About to look them in the eyes and laugh while he lied to them. And the thing is—it wasn't the lies. It was the ease. How easily he moved from my world to theirs. As if he owned all of it.

And then I realized: oh yeah. I could hate him.

I don't expect you to look at him and see what I see. I get how that can seem distant to you. But the rest of it— the swagger, privilege masquerading as luck, blond hair and nice leather. You can see that, can't you? The Lyman Hunters of the world pay you to let yourself be fucked, Alex. They don't know a world that isn't about fucking or paying. And that—that alone—a history of that . . .

Isn't that worth punishment?

The Moors

Two sisters and a dog live out their lives on the bleak English moors, and dream of love and power. The arrival of a hapless governess and a moor-hen set all three on a strange and dangerous path. The Moors *is a dark comedy about love, desperation, and visibility. Huldey is the youngest sister, a would-be author, and is choking on her own invisibility. In this speech, Huldey reads from her diary. The interruption of the family dog provides her with an audience of one, in front of whom she briefly thrives . . . and then crashes.*

HULDEY: Monday: I am very unhappy.

Tuesday: It is bleak here, and I am unhappy.

Wednesday: There was fog, and my digestive system was disagreeable, and I was greatly unhappy.

Thursday: I hate Agatha.

(The mastiff enters. He looks at Huldey.)

Go away. I'm reading my diary, and it is very very private, well if you insist, but just a little bit!

(She reads to him:)

Friday: There is nothing good in the world.

Saturday: I am very unhappy, and there is a driving rain on the moors, and today a governess arrived, and I think we shall be best friends, closer than sisters.

Sunday: There was sun, briefly, and it left, and I was unhappy, and Agatha will ruin the governess the way she always ruins everything.

Monday: I had a dream. There was a great hulking awful man, and he came into my bedchamber, and I said, "Go away! Go away!" and he did not go away. I was briefly happy.

(She looks at the mastiff. He looks back. No longer reading from the diary, a sort of free-style aria that becomes more and more urgent:)

Everybody always wants to know what I am thinking. It's hard to be rather well-known. I wouldn't say *famous*— but someone else might. Whenever I go to the village, everybody says, "There is the parson's youngest daughter." They say, "I wonder what exciting thing she is thinking today!" They say, "I hear she's a famous writer." And one doesn't like to be talked about all the time, it makes one feel quite uncomfortable, so I say, "Oh stop, I'm just like you, there's nothing special about me at all." And they just *refuse* to believe me. They think I'm special. They think it's so very evident, when they look at me, that I was destined for wonderful things, even if I can't see those things myself, it's so very evident to every last one of them.

(Beat.
Huldey bursts into tears.)

The Roommate

Recently divorced and living in an old house in Iowa, Sharon finds a sensible roommate like herself—a woman in her fifties—to make ends meet. But she quickly learns that Robyn is a former con artist, fleeing from her past—and couldn't be further from the ladies in Sharon's book club. As both women become close, each recognizes in the other an overwhelming desire to transform her own life. But the only question is: What will be the price of that transformation? A dark comedy about what it takes to re-route your life—and what happens when the wheels come off.

In the following sequence, Robin has taught Sharon how to scam people over the phone, and Sharon targets Tanya, a particularly simple woman who runs the weekly book club. As Sharon makes this call, we see her come fully alive.

SHARON *(In a French accent)*:
>Hello?
>Yes, is this Tanya?
>Tanya, hello, this is
>Juliette
>DuBois
>from The Franco-Global Association for International
>>Orphans
>based in Normandy, France
>Yes
>Normandy is a lovely city
>there are stone walls and it is right next to the ocean
>and long ago people stormed the beaches with great
>>passion

(Robyn clears her throat—"Hurry up!"—and Sharon takes the cue.)

>—which is all to say
>I wonder if you are interested in saving the lives of
>>starving children
>orphans, *oui*, orphans

in Senegal
in many places, but specifically Senegal
have you been?
it's lovely
the bright colors, the drums, the hats
yes, Senegal is a place of music and motion and hats
and children without parents
—What?
well
what we do is, we provide orphans with things they
    generally lack
like *pain au chocolat*
and bicycles
and vegetables
and small hats
and the right kinds of love.
And love requires money.
All kinds of love, but especially the right kinds.
There can be no love of any kinds
without money.

(*Beat. This comes from a personal place.*

   *Sharon thinks about her life as she speaks, and she gets
emotional, and it's actually weirdly honest and raw.*)

Think about what it is to be alone.
It is a late night somewhere
wherever you are
and you are alone.
Think about the objects you arrange around you.
But everything is cold under your hand.
And then someone comes into your life.
And you become different.
You find yourself to be . . . truly . . . alive.
Think about how one person can change an entire
    lifetime
of accumulated coldness and objects and silence.

(Beat. Tanya is affected by this and wants to help. Sharon makes direct eye contact with Robyn as she seals the deal, speaking with a quiet and inarguable victory:)

Thank you, Tanya.
It's people like you who make the difference.
The next step requires your date of birth
and your credit card information.

CHARISE CASTRO SMITH

Feathers and Teeth

Following the death of her mother (Ellie) two months prior to this scene, thirteen-year-old Chris's life has become a living nightmare. Her father, Arthur, has fallen under the spell of his new girlfriend, Carol, and Chris is left alone to deal with her overwhelming grief. In the following scene, alone late at night in her living room, she tells the story of her parent's meeting in an attempt to assuage her loneliness, and with a distant hope that the story will draw forth some sort of sign from her dead mother.

CHRIS:

      Once upon a time, many many years ago in 1963,
      A girl named Ellie lived in a little factory town in the
          Midwest
      With her mom and dad, nana and gramps.

      (Very faintly, an animation starts to appear in the kitchen window, sketches that follow the story that Chris is telling. The drawings are flowing and vivid, slightly childlike but

with a great deal of sorrow in them. Like a Chagall, or one of Lorca's sketches.)

> More than anything, Ellie loved to sing and play the guitar.
> But Nana and Gramps thought she ought to go to secretary school.
> So one night, Ellie kissed her sleeping parents good-bye
> And she got on a bus bound for San Francisco, California.

> When she got there, she got a job in a bookstore during the day.
> But every night she would go to a coffee place and sing and play the guitar onstage.

> Then one night, a soldier named Arthur was on his way home from the war in Vietnam.
> And on his way home, he stopped in San Francisco.
> And one night while he was in San Francisco, he went to a coffee place.
> And in that coffee place, he saw Ellie and heard her sing.

> And he fell in love with her at first sight.

(Animation Arthur falls in love with animation Ellie at first sight.)

> And so he decided not to go straight home to the Midwest, where Arthur also was from.

> Instead, he stayed in San Francisco and tried to get Ellie to go out on a date with him.
> And Ellie didn't really want to go on a date with him at first because Arthur could be a real square sometimes, but finally Ellie saw that Arthur had a warm smile

And was very persistent and so finally she said yes to
  a date,
And two weeks later they got married in San
  Francisco.

Then Ellie got pregnant,
And so they came back to the Midwest because their
  families wanted to be around
Ellie's baby, which was me.

(Chris closes her eyes and focuses hard.)

Mom? Are you there?
This is your daughter, Christine.
If your spirit is present, Ellie, please make that presence
  known somehow.
Ellie, this is your daughter Christine.
I love you and miss you so much.
If your spirit is present, Ellie, please give me a sign.

Mom?

RUBY RAE SPIEGEL

Dry Land

Dry Land is a play about girls, abortion, female friendship, resiliency, and what happens in one high school locker room after everybody's left. Ester is a swimmer trying to stay afloat. In this scene, she waits with Victor in a dorm room hallway, after being locked out by his roommate. Victor tells her about the time he kissed her best friend, Amy.

VICTOR: Okay. Um. Well last year we kissed at a party. I was a freshman, here, and she was in tenth grade I guess, then. I was at the party because I couldn't sleep. It was my dad's birthday the day before that's why I was home, and I just felt so . . . Anyway, we made out in the yard. She didn't want to go any further and that was fine with me, I just wanted some company I guess. But after we kissed for like five minutes, like not long at all, she said she wanted me to walk in there and tell everyone that she gave me head and that I came all over her face. I thought that was really weird. She seemed so sad and anxious, like she wasn't even interested in me but like in proving something. But

I did. I really couldn't tell you why but I told my friend who was there who I guess told the other people who were there and the girl whose house it was kicked her out. I remember the look on her face when the girl kicked her out, calling her ah, calling her a bitch and stuff like that. She flipped everyone off and then she wiped her face with the palm of her hand. Like a big wipe like this. *(He demonstrates)* I don't know. That's why I said that. But maybe she is a slut now, I really wouldn't know. I just go down to see my brother.

SUSAN SOON HE STANTON

Today Is My Birthday

Emily is a would-be writer whose bubble life in New York City has popped. Finding life back home chaotic and unfulfilling, she becomes strangely activated after creating a sassy alter-ego for a radio bit. Told through a playful mixture of live radio, voicemail, and phone calls, Today Is My Birthday *is a quirky comedy about life with a thousand friends on Facebook and no one to have dinner with on Saturday night.*

This speech takes place when Emily drunk-dials her ex-fiancé, Sebastian, and leaves a voicemail.

EMILY: Hey Sebastian. It's Emily. I was just calling to see how you are. I've started acting. On the radio? It feels kind of natural for me, actually. Because most of the time, I can't stand myself at all. Like, not the sound of my voice or my thoughts, or the cadence of my steps. I don't mean that in a self-deprecating way. I just. —When you broke up with me via text message, I was crossing Houston Street and got hit by a car. Not like, terribly so, but you know, it happened. So I ran into the subway before the driver could get out. And I started crying. Just really hard. Not from you breaking up with me but from the shock of being hit by a car. Sitting across from me was an old, steely-looking man. I want to say he was a priest but he probably wasn't, since it was two in the morning. Just before he got off the train, he took me by the shoulders, looked into my eyes and said, "Don't cry on the subway. You hear? Don't cry on the subway." I think he's my guardian angel. I just wanted you to know, I've met a wonderful man. His name is Keoni. So you can stop worrying about me, because I don't worry about you. But if something's wrong, you can always let me know. I'm here for you.

KATE TARKER

An Almanac for Farmers and Lovers in Mexico

Flora and Pelé were eager for their Mexican wedding, until Pelé transformed into a bird. Flora and her friends have diverse reactions to this incident. Flora, for her part, is keeping the groom in a little cage, negotiating with the judge, and trying to piece her cosmos back together. In this speech, San Cristóbal (the patron saint of travel) narrates an asteroid narrowly missing Earth, while Molly, Flora's maid of honor, tries to ask for condoms in Spanish at the local pharmacy.

SAN CRISTÓBAL:
> Let's check in on the meteorological conditions.
> On that fateful and fateless night in history
> As Molly was trying to muster up the courage to ask
>   for what she wanted—
>
> What she really wanted—
>
> There was indeed, an asteroid.
> It was the size of a golf ball and it was hurtling
>   through space.

No it was a meteor the size of a golf course.
No it was a cosmic joke the size of a school bus.

At any rate, the asteroid was hurtling straight for
    Earth.
If it landed, life as we know it would be wiped out
For ages and eons.
For a few years at least.
For a nanosecond
A petrified nanosecond—

Hurtle hurtle hurtle hurtle
In their final moment as a species,
Coincidentally coinciding with the predicted year of
    the Mayan apocalypse,
All of human kind would laugh.

The impact from the extraterrestrial rock would make
    room for entirely new beginnings
New forms
New kinds of art
New genres of science
New languages emanating from knees
Of course "knees" isn't the right word for it, neither is
    "language"
The United States would no longer be tyrannized by
    the two-party system
Global inequality would not even be the faintest
    memory
Ice cream would no longer drip down anyone's wrists
    in the summer
Architecture from the seventies would no longer
    offend anyone's sensibilities.

This was the change people had been longing for,
That had been promised but never delivered by an
    endless parade of politicians
Something new under a slowly dying sun

Something really radical
Accidental extinction
Of Man and iPhone alike
Reborn as unprecedented *animalitos* roaming the planet
Animalitos not governed by propriety and politeness
Or by what they learned about social hierarchies in
    endless schooling
No, the members of the new species would be:
True anarchists.

STEPHANIE TIMM

Tails of Wasps

A hotel room. Deborah and Frank are holed up, hiding from the press.

DEBORAH:

Well

I've always been a proponent of legalizing prostitution

Haven't I always been a proponent of legalizing
prostitution I mean

If men have not evolved past a compulsive
biologically based need for sexual variety

If under their suits and ties men are just animals
unconsciously compelled to sow their seeds Then
why shouldn't women get to benefit

Why shouldn't women get to profit Why should we
be victimized Vandalized

Scandalized

Legalize it and regulate it

That way hookers won't end up giving all their
proceeds to pimps Or better yet

Women and girls won't be trafficked from destitute
    and collapsed states then forced into
sex slavery
Why shouldn't women get to capitalize on this entire
    industry of lust
But don't stop with legalization or we'd end up being
    a magnet for sex trafficking No
We need to go further
Let there be labor laws and protections Let it be a career
    path
Let them unionize
Let them have health insurance retirement benefits
Paid vacation even for god's sake
If only having a quick fuck with someone you're not
    married to could be a Clean
Safe
Unemotional transaction Take the shame out of it
There'd be no more shame in it than getting your hair
    cut or getting your clothes dry-cleaned I mean let's
    face it
Keeping it illegal punishes the victims
Keeping it illegal is the equivalent of saying it doesn't
    exist And it exists
Oh it exists and it is thriving
Growing like a fucking cancer Make it legal and every-
    body wins
Prostitutes win because they make some money
Men win because they can openly satiate their sexual
    appetites with less shame then getting a Quarter
    Pounder with Cheese at McDonald's
Wives win because nobody is judging them for having
    a husband who needs to part more
than one pair of thighs
Only mistresses will lose but shame on them Shame
    on mistresses
It's practically polygamy but without the wife's
    consent and let's face it

Polygamy is just another form of slavery So anyway
    THANK YOU Frank
I'm grateful at least that you didn't go that route But
    I do wonder
by the way
What's the matter with having a lap dance then
    jerking off afterwards Why isn't that enough
But anyway
My point
I believe in legalizing prostitution I buy into that and
Some day I'll run for office myself and that'll be my
    platform
In a theoretical world where the physical can be
    separate from the emotional from the psychological
I would be okay with you having a series of call girls
    but as it is Things being what they are
A sex scandal is the worst possible thing to happen to a
    man in politics Especially a married man in politics
And the only one it's worse for is HIS WIFE GOD
    BLESS AMERICA.

MFONISO UDOFIA

Sojourners

Sojourners *is the first play in the Ufot Family Cycle. This play, a drama in two acts, follows three immigrants (Nigerian/Ibibio) and an African-American woman as they attempt to navigate Houston, Texas, in 1978. This speech by Ukpong Ekpeyoung, the boisterous and deeply irresponsible husband of Abasiama Ekpeyoung (eight months pregnant) takes place in their small Houston home. This is Ukpong's return speech after he abandoned his heavily pregnant wife to experience his first American rally.*

UKPONG: Eh-heh! Softsoft. Hey now, my softsoft, look my way. *(Kiss)* Let me tell you what happened. After you hear, you will totally forgive this your husband. First. I am sorry. Believe. I am. But a miracle happened and. Sit, there for me now. This is a powerful tale.

(Ukpong marshals Abasiama onto the couch.)

Some days ago, Etuk and I—we went in that his Thunderbird. The one his father just bought him. We were riding, like our normal okay. Testing horsepower, and then something came on network radio. A.M. This—a social . . . I don't recall the correct name. A sort of gathering. A kind of meeting—no, yes, wait—they call it "rally"! A rally where people come to talk about our world. It was advertised! I mean, why not? How do I pass over, Ama? I was the one who told Etuk to drive to the concourse and get on that freeway. We get there and—hey! Just like the radio foretold. All of these people. People like you have never ever seen. Houston?! Hm. You couldn't imagine it. Whites. Blacks. Hispanic. Asian. Women. Poor. Rich. Who could have thought all of these sorts of people jam-packed in one room? And we rallied about everything. Oh. Politics? Economy? Love? No subject taboo! And then this speaker! Sampson. This man got up there, 'round midnight, to light the altar on fire on how we have to live and love and that that is the sole purpose of life. It blew my mind. The whole process blew my mind to shards. This kind of peace. This kind of living. Living initiated from a radio? Remember radio back home? An instrument of death. No good news ever came out of that thing just consistent alarmalarmalarm. Radio Nigeria only broadcasts Kalashnikov fire. But here?! *(Sucks his teeth)* Never have I seen anything like it. No guns, no thought of a shot being fired. Watch! Americans have the way of it! They have the human understanding! We didn't stop—didn't think about stopping until four–five A.M. And then everyone went for some drink and it was cool. Nothing but cool. Listen. Even Etuk, with his impatience? Once there? That man sat entranced.

PAULA VOGEL

Don Juan Comes Home from Iraq

Don Juan Comes Home from Iraq *is a play that follows the journey of Marine Captain Don Juan, who comes to Philadelphia seeking Sergeant Cressida Morrison, a woman he loves whom he has wronged. He has been a profligate womanizer who has slept with the army women who were assigned to him in Iraq. It is a journey that takes place in Juan's mind the second he is airborne when an IED explodes. His company of three men and three women play all the characters.*

> *(Cressida, late at night, drinking straight out of a whiskey bottle. She writes a letter:)*

CRESSIDA: I probably shouldn't send this letter to you. I've been sending you a letter a week for the past two months and: No Answer. Do you have any idea how exhausting it is for a girl to be pithy, sexy, saucy, teasing in one page and a thirty-three-cent stamp?

Did they deploy you to the moon, Captain Darling?

So. Tonight I went to a bar. Heels, a little scoop neck, a touch of rouge. By my third shot of whiskey, I thought, Oh, why not? On my fourth shot I thought, All right, He's kinda cute. Four shots are enough to say okay, yes, let's go to your house. Four shots are enough to still be sensate to a man's tongue.

A lesson every woman should know: Never take a man home who has had more whiskey than you. He's asleep on your side of the bed. His mouth is open—as if he's still searching for the tit. Sweet.

I am bored out of my fucking mind, damn you. I'm on my fifth shot now. I am definitely going to send this to you.

What the hell did you do to my body? I used to be a sweet girl, I used to whisper in bed: "Oh. Oh. That's so nice." I used to moan with great politeness. They all believed me.

The *noises* you forced out of my mouth! I still don't know if I was crying because you released me, lover, or because you invaded me. You . . . you turned on some, some switch and now I am voracious. Fuck You! You have turned me into a carnivore in a city without meat.

I know I'm never going to see you again, Captain Darling. You are treating me like every other girl you pick up in a bar, and goddamn it, I was more than that and you fucking know it! So I have nothing to lose.

Wherever you are, Captain Darling, I hope you cannot sleep.

Love,

Cressida

KATHRYN WALAT

Romeo & Naomi Ramirez

Anna (mid-twenties) is a rookie cop on her first undercover narcotics assignment at a school in South Florida. Under the name Naomi Ramirez she poses as a high school senior, attracting the attention of honors student Jesus (pronounced HEH-soos) Romeo. Earlier in this scene Anna's boyfriend Josh revealed that he slept with a female acquaintance from high school; he is now apologizing for everything under the sun. That shitty news, together with the mounting pressure to deliver on an arrest, drives Anna to reveal details of the dangerous role she is playing, and eventually, to seek Josh's advice.

ANNA: Don't fucking apologize, Josh. I hate it when you apologize over stupid shit. I need to you *listen*, okay?

So there's this kid—this guy—he's eighteen. His name's Romeo—I'm not shitting you—*Jesus* Romeo in fact and he's . . . amazing. And quite possibly the biggest player in South Florida—or not, I don't know.

He wants to join the Coast Guard—to-to *help* people—and he's an honors student and like crazy into Shakespeare, and he wants to take me to the prom, okay? Today in school he sang me a song—right before class started—in front of *McShane*'s class, Romeo is serenading me *a capella* and everyone is watching—but unlike when all of them were watching me fuck up my sonnet, this time they're cheering him on!

And it's like kamikaze—*everyone* is going to see him crash and burn—because that's also when he decides to ask me to the prom, and I'm like: Seriously? In front of class you are doing this?

That's right, it takes balls. And you know what else? It's exactly—textbook—what they tell you *not* to do when you're undercover. Don't attract attention. Do *not* get involved with the civilians, never mind possible targets.

But in that moment—and this is the crazy thing—I *did* want to go to the prom with him. That's totally what I wanted to do. And I have goose bumps all over, and my heart is beating like *crazy*—it was like I was back in high school, except better, because for once *I'm* the girl being serenaded and—in that moment, my heart said *yes*.

I said I would *think about it*. What was I supposed to say?

And then—*then*—McShane made everyone sit down and open our books. And then. I lean in—because he's sitting at the desk right next to me, there in the back row—and I whisper, "Hey, so—about that weed? . . ."

And he says, "Don't worry, I'll have it for you tomorrow."

See Bat Fly

Melanie (late thirties) is a biologist who researches bats, and suffers from increasingly terrifying nightmares. As Christmas approaches, she finds herself transplanted from Boston to Albuquerque, where she undergoes treatment at a radical sleep clinic, and tries to reconnect with her nerdy physicist brother. Here, Melanie is being uncharacteristically revealing to Jack, the short-order cook and self-

declared shaman at a rundown diner off Route 66. It's the middle
of the night. Jack's got nothing but time. He listens, then extends
his hand and says, "Come with me." Melanie takes it, and they go
to the desert.

MELANIE: So I've been driving. All night. Up and down Route
66—and the way it cuts right through the city, a straight
line—mountains to the east—over that flat land that
keeps going and going, out into . . . America.

Past the motels, and I'm imagining those tiny rooms—
cable-TV, beds of sleeping people. VACANCY. All that
neon—green and red—so bright, against the night sky.
I can almost pretend it's another time and place—a sim-
pler time—and that's comforting for a little while but.

My butt aches from driving. And it's a stupid waste of
gas. And if I hear Bing Crosby's "White Christmas" one
more time, I might lose it. And it feels really good to be
here with you, and eat something—and just . . . *not* move.

I get nightmares. Especially this one—it comes to me,
again and again. Sometimes a few nights will go by and
I'll think maybe it's gone, I start to relax into bed, but—

I can't outrun it. Even in Albuquerque.

I'm standing on this flat place, high up—the sun is
so bright, almost blinding. And when I look down I'm
wearing these white canvas shoes like my mom used to
wear, and they're covered with red dust, and I'm thinking, "Isn't that strange?" And suddenly.

Suddenly the earth drops out from under my feet,
and I fall—my stomach lurches—but I grab hold of this
branch with one hand, but I'm slipping, and it's tearing
my skin, and blood is running down my bare arm—I'm
naked—and my other hand is clawing the air—because
I know, if I fall—I'll be *trapped*—and I'm never, ever going
to find a way out. And then.

TIMBERLAKE WERTENBAKER

Jefferson's Garden

Jefferson's Garden *is a play about a young Quaker, Christian, who joins the American Revolution. He meets Thomas Jefferson in Virginia and falls in love with Susannah, a slave who works at the Raleigh Tavern. After fighting against the British, Christian finds Thomas Jefferson again and remains enthralled by him. He marries a niece of James Madison and discovers he now lives in a world very far from the ideals of freedom for which he first abandoned his Quaker home. The following monologue is from Act One, Scene 11:*

> *(George Mason and Thomas Jefferson are at the Raleigh Tavern in Williamsburg, Virginia, just before the Revolution. Christian has come down from Maryland to hear them. Nelly Rose sweeps in with her son, James Madison, in tow. She is about fifty, very gracious, very Southern, and unstoppable.)*

NELLY ROSE: Dear George, what a trip we've had. All we hear is talk of revolution and what *is* Patrick Henry doing looking so military out there? He hardly had the courtesy to greet us but then he was always a ne'er-do-well—stay away from him, James, the man can't farm, went bankrupt, almost ruined the family and killed his poor mother with worry, and now he thinks just because he took the bar in six weeks he can run the Revolution. Tom, how is dear Martha? I haven't seen her since you've hidden her away in that mountaintop of yours. She was always such a delicate creature but such a good dancer. *(She spots Christian)* And who are you, young man? Have you traveled from the North like my son? And now I must introduce James. He's just come down from Princeton but it's taken us a long time to get here because James would stop and ask everyone what was going on. He calls it studying the mood of the place, well, it doesn't take a lot of conversation to know the mood of Virginia, you can pick it up by just feeling, but he's studied in Princeton so he doesn't understand feeling. Well Jim, what did you find out?

CALAMITY WEST

Give It All Back

Give It All Back *is a two-act comedy set in a Paris hotel room in the 1960s; this monologue takes place in the final scene of the play. Here we find the character of The Artist being interviewed by Patsy Peifer with* Time Magazine. *Up until this part of the play, The Artist has had the comfort (and at times discomfort) of hiding behind the shine of his persona. Patsy Peifer, however, has chosen to expertly dismantle this persona through the course of her interview. Here's what The Artist has to say about it.*

THE ARTIST:

We're here to talk about my music, okay?

That's it.

So cut the personal shit.

And that includes *your* personal shit.

You saw me in Greenwich Village? I didn't see you
    there.

I didn't see none of you people there.

Yet here you are, sitting across from me,

telling me you had the balls to call my *mother*?

My birth certificate's in your *bag*?
I've never even seen my birth certificate.
But Lord Almighty! Here it is!
In Patsy Peifer's bag,
in Paris,
in 1966.

You think I'm stupid?
I'm not stupid.
People like you? You're the stupid ones.
Not me.
And you can all go to hell.
And I'll go to Heaven.
Then you'll see.

I hate this.
I hate this.
I hate this.
I hate this.

I don't want this.
I want something . . . normal.
But what would I even do with that?
I couldn't get a job . . . anywhere.
This is the only thing I can do and it fucking . . .
    blows . . .
And what is all of this gonna look like next year, ten
    years, twenty years from now?
It's gonna look like a mess.
That's what it's gonna look like.
Which is the *opposite of normal*.

I wanna go home.
I want to go home.
I want to go home.
I just want to go home.

LEAH NANAKO WINKLER

Kentucky

Adam, twenties, talks to himself and the audience before attending a wedding rehearsal dinner with Hiro, his high school crush.

ADAM: I miss how handsome I used to be. I miss how effortless everything seemed and was.

   I miss playing. And grabbing a rebound on the basketball court. The feeling of leather on my palms. And the sound of my name echoing in a gymnasium I miss enthusiasm.

   And desire. The feeling of desire. For the moment. For the future. For every girl I meet. I miss gliding through the hallways unaware of my own beauty as my limbs— they moved me effortlessly from classroom to classroom to practice to my car, and I would drive it, the windows down while the air tussled my hair. And I would be *so handsome*. I mean, I'm not a bad-looking guy now. Sure. But back then? Shit. Was I handsome! And now I miss it like I miss drinking alcohol without regret and going fast without consequence. And dancing hard unaware that there might not be a tomorrow.

I miss my best friend D.J., who died of a heroin overdose. I miss not thinking.

These days I'm thinking that I should have worked harder. Tried harder. Took better care of my hair—I hope it doesn't thin like my father's—will I . . . still be attractive with hair that is receding? Should I take medication? Gee I hope my belly doesn't swell. And my feet do they smell and my teeth. Darn. I hope, I hope. I hope I hope I hope I hope. I hope I wont have to spend so many more nights alone listening to Jewel and Joni Mitchell while staring at the stars up above and wishing and wishing and wishing for love!

BESS WOHL

Small Mouth Sounds

The entire play takes place at a silent spiritual retreat in Upstate New York. In this monologue, the guru's mandate of silence has been temporarily lifted to allow the participants in the retreat to ask "brief" questions. Here, Ned stands at a microphone, addressing his question to the guru.

NED *(Clears his throat)*: Hello. Thank you for taking my question. First I want to thank my fellow—retreaters—for the great questions everyone's brought up so far. I know it's only been a few days but my mind is like . . . *(Makes a gesture for "blown")* So . . .

(He clears his throat again. Laughs self-consciously. Nobody else does.)

On that note, I can't really stand here without acknowledging . . . Wow. You've changed my life. I just, I love your books and tapes, and, and it's an honor to be standing here. In front of you. I basically think you're a total rock star, so . . . I kind of wanted to put that out there.

Um . . . So, where to begin.

My question is sort of . . . Big. It's, well, you know how—there's the planet. Earth. And then there's—okay, you know what, let me back up for a second here—I promise not to give you my life story. But . . . Just to give you a tiny little bit about where I'm coming from—I've always been an outdoor enthusiast? Then—quick sidebar—about four and a half years ago, I fell while rock climbing and shattered my skull in eight places. I just have, you know, it looks . . . *(Gestures to his head)* Without the hat, you can tell.

I survived—obviously—which was pretty much a miracle, truly, although I still have trouble remembering certain things. Like the day of the week sometimes—which I think is pretty common, right? And how I like my coffee—which can be more, you know, not that it's a big deal. That's generally, like, an easy process of trial and error.

Anyway, cutting to the chase, I was in the hospital for about two years, during which I lost my job at a major marketing firm—and also my wife started sleeping with my little brother although of course I wasn't aware of it at the time. Then the week I got out of the hospital I was the victim of an armed robbery in which they took, you know, my wallet, credit cards, social-security card, which led to my identity ultimately being stolen, even though I wasn't aware of that at the time either, but later, after my house burned down, um, long story, I became aware that I have bad credit due to the identity theft and also some loans that I took out for my brother, who is a recovering heroin addict and also a "musician." I gave him the money before I knew he was sleeping with my wife, obviously.

(A moment to recover.)

So yeah, I got divorced. Then both of my parents died, six months apart. I started drinking. I had thoughts of suicide that were, well pretty much constant? Then, another miracle, I got in the program, got sober, stopped wanting to kill myself—but after that, ironically, my sponsor killed himself—by walking into traffic on the Long Island Expressway. That was last year. The same thing actually happened to my dog. Hit by a car, I mean. That was a month later. I don't mean to equate the two. I just think it's weird, the, like, synchronicities and patterns and stuff that are everywhere, you know, if you look for them.

I have my health. Except for the intermittent short-term memory loss. Which, given everything, may actually be a blessing.

And right, as I was saying, I got a new job—well, it's volunteer, for now—at this place Earthwatch, it's an environmental—and it's just that, at Earthwatch it's just like, become very clear that . . . With what's happening . . .

With the planet . . .

Well, just one example, there's like, not going to be enough food left in fifty years.

Crops are going to die out, because of drought and stuff.

And there's two billion more people projected to be on the planet by then, which means we'll have to somehow find more land to farm, which means even more trees will be cut down, which means with the greenhouse effect everything will just get even hotter—and so we're talking mass migrations of people, wars over dwindling resources, species going extinct—and the coral reefs are going, and the polar ice caps . . .

And anyway—it's all going to be gone. It really is the end of the world. At least as we know it. So much suffering is in store, you know? It just is. And the truth is, it may be too late. I mean, it probably is already too late to do anything about it.

And, so, I mean my intention is just to breathe and find peace with all of this.

Stay in the present, you know . . . Stay present . . .

But I keep feeling like we should be, like, *doing* something—or—

I mean, maybe we *shouldn't* be at peace, and just sitting around *breathing*, because the world is—like, fucked, so—sorry.

Or, like, maybe this is just all my mind analyzing too much. I know this is just a story I'm telling . . . And anyway, it's all an illusion. I think.

And this is probably just my ego talking. If I could just wake up to enlightenment maybe I would understand that . . . That . . . None of this matters, but . . . I think I'm not really. I think I'm . . . I think I'm . . . Wondering . . . Given everything . . . You know, everything . . .

(He suddenly looks very lost.)

What was my question?

(Under his breath, but the microphone just barely picks it up:)

Shit.

LAUREN YEE

King of the Yees

For nearly twenty years, playwright Lauren Yee's father, Larry, has been a driving force in the Yee Family Association, a seemingly obsolescent Chinese-American men's club formed one hundred and fifty years ago in the wake of the Gold Rush. But when her father goes missing, Lauren must plunge into the rabbit hole of San Francisco Chinatown and confront a world both foreign and familiar. King of the Yees *is an epic joyride across cultural, national, and familial borders, and explores what it means to truly be a Yee.*

> *(Larry Yee talks to the audience just as the arrest of his political mentor, Leland Yee, hits the afternoon news:)*

LARRY *(To us)*:

> My daughter's out feeding her meter.
> She told me to tell you she'll be right back.
> She also told me I'm not supposed to tell you
>   anything else, so— ("Zip!")
> I gotta go soon anyway, get ready for the dinner, find
>   the Doc.

That's Leland.

He calls me Larry.

I call him Doc.

We're pretty tight.

I remember the first election I did with Leland. Supervisor's race.

He called me up, night before the election, he told me,
"Larry, you gotta go on 19th Avenue, take down all
those other guys' signs, and put up mine."

And I said, "Okay, Doc. Don't you worry. *(As Yogi
Bear)* Larry Yee is on the case!"

And the next day,

All of 19th Avenue is just "YEE,"

one after the other.

"YEE."

"YEE."

"YEE."

I'm not saying I won it for him, but my dad always
used to say, having your name up there, that's
pretty important.

And growing up, my dad knew everything.

(Bang.

Where is that coming from? The red double doors?)

Lauren?

No?

Who is it?

Nobody here but us chickens.

I mean, Yees.

I mean, *Wongs*.

*(An unseen old TV mounted in the ceiling corner turns on.
Larry looks up.)*

Oh hey, there's Leland. We made the afternoon news!

Hey, Doc!

Wonder where he is.

And look! The Association! They got a picture of us!
Wow.

(Larry takes out a remote.)

Lemme turn up the volume.

The Tiger Among Us

For Lia and her ghetto wannabe brother, Pao, being the only Hmong kids in town is tough; it's even tougher when that town happens to be in outstate Minnesota. And when a stranger's arrival in the midst of hunting season threatens their tenuous existence, Lia finds herself caught between her family and her dreams in this modern-day Midwestern folktale about a Hmong-American family and the tenuous bonds that tie us all together. Pao speaks to a class of ninth graders as part of Asian History Month. Classroom, May 1995.

PAO:
　　　Okay.
　　　So.
　　　My name's Pao.
　　　You can call me Mr. P.
　　　That's cool, too, if you want.
　　　Ms. G's out moving her car, but she said I should
　　　　　probably get started.
　　　. . .
　　　Okay. So. Hmong.
　　　Everyone, they wanna know what Hmong is,
　　　Everyone around here, they like, what the fuck
　　　—'scuse my mouth—
　　　But they like, fuck, it's cold up in here and we're
　　　　　freezing our asses off and there're all these tropical
　　　　　Asians showing up, I thought we were all blond up
　　　　　in here.
　　　So I can tell you what Hmong is

but it's like real secret.
Like I'mma kill you secret.
No shit.
Okay, so Hmong, we come from a bunch of different
    countries.
We ain't got no, like, Hmong country,
guess 'cause nobody likes us.
Which I get
—I don't like me either, story of my life—
And we're from all over.
We're in China
and then fucking Chinese
—no offense, nobody's Chinese?—
Fucking Chinese, they're like fuck you.
So we go down to Laos.
And fucking Laos
—or Laotians—
they're also like fuck you and they try to kill us
BUT THEY CAN'T!
'Cause we're TROPICAL SURVIVORS!
With the TIGERS and LIONS and flesh-eating
    MONKEYS!
We hunt those dudes for breakfast.
We eat tiger for breakfast!
Tony-the-Tiger kind!
'Cause we're CIA motherfuckers!
You ever hear this shit? About how the American
    Government recruited Hmong guys to fight the
    Viet Kong for them,
'Cause I guess Asian-on-Asian violence is cheaper.
OH! And we eat snake. For the protein.
We bite the shit out of them headfirst and swallow
    the whole thing up.
They're like noodles to us:
Snake ramen.
That's our Thanksgiving dinner.
People're like, "Oh, yeah, turkey,"
And we're like, "Oh, yeah, snake."

(Pao makes a snake-eating/slurping gesture/noise. Thao enters the room, wheels in his garbage bin unit.)

Naw, I'm just playing!
We don't really eat snake.

(Thao noisily empties the trash can. Pao tries not to look at Thao. Thao finishes, wheels his garbage unit out of the room.)

We have big families.
And we eat a lot.
I figure that's like everyone else, but what do I know.

STEFANIE ZADRAVEC

Colony Collapse

Set in rural Oregon against the contemporary plagues of meth addiction, missing children, and a failing ecology, ex-felon Mark (forties) and ex-junkie Julia (thirties) have taken over the day-to-day operations of an orchard. With no farming experience, the couple quickly realizes that they are in over their heads, but they forge ahead believing that if they can produce a viable crop, a new beginning is possible. The couple's efforts are thwarted when the search for a missing fifteen-year-old girl leads police to their property. At the same time, Mark's estranged son, Jason (eighteen), mysteriously shows up in the middle of the night, unearthing old wounds and new suspicions.

In this scene, Mark came to tell his son that he needs to pack up and go, but instead they hash out the events that sent Mark to prison four years ago. When Jason was thirteen he used Mark's passcode and stole the deposit bag from Land's End where Mark was a store manager. He just wanted to get his dad in trouble. Mark knew Jason framed him for the crime but took the heat, because although they were not close he couldn't turn in his thirteen-year-old son. Now he repeatedly asks Jason why he did it. Jason finally admits that he was mad, because he didn't have a winter coat, even though his father worked at Land's End. Mark has just realized that he spent four years in prison for a Class-B felony, because his son needed a forty-five dollar parka. But instead of stealing a parka, he took twelve thousand dollars in cash. Jason insists he had no idea there would be twelve thousand dollars in the bag. He thought maybe five hundred dollars. I mean, who shops at Land's End?

Here Jason says, I wish I could take it all back, you have no idea . . . *And Mark unloads:*

MARK: No, *you have no idea,* I can't get work.

And I don't have any money, so now I can't pay for this, this, *jerk* with his precious bees, so despite Julia's romantic notions of *the family farm,* we really can't afford any of this right now—

And I can't . . . vote, which is fine, I don't care about that, but it makes the point.

I'm a second-class human being now.

And I get it.

I wasn't a very good human being to start off with, but my god, Jason, Julia lost her friggin' marbles.

I tell you, there are days when I'm tempted to think I don't love her anymore—*that's between you and me by the way—*

But then I think about what happened to her . . . how she was when I found her.

This horrible place she was staying. Men all over her.

That *I do* take responsibility for.

I can't take back what those years did to her.

ANNA ZIEGLER

Boy

Boy *is the coming-of-age story of a young man who grew up in very, shall we say, unique circumstances. We meet Adam as a twenty-three-year-old man, but soon see that his inability to move forward is directly connected to his inability to come to terms with his past— specifically that for fifteen years, after a circumcision accident, he was raised as a girl. The play is based on a true story, one from which I diverged particularly when it comes to the character of the doctor who treated Adam. In my play Wendell is well-meaning, driven less by personal agenda than love for the child. So it is difficult for Adam finally to reveal to Wendell how deeply he failed him. Adam begins by forcing Wendell to read aloud a letter he wrote a long time ago but never sent.*

WENDELL: Dear Wendell, here's something I never told you. When we were kids, Stephen and me, we shared a room. You didn't want that, but my parents couldn't afford a bigger house, so that's the way it was.

(Wendell looks up but Adam motions that he continue.)

And I remember all these nights, too many to count, when we were going to sleep and Stephen maybe thought I was asleep already or maybe he didn't give a shit, and he was ten maybe eleven when it started.

I watched him; I saw how everything worked. How his dick would get hard in his hand, how he caressed it like it was the softest sweetest thing in the world and then how he fought it, like an animal trying to break free. And when he came, I swear I felt it too . . . this sensation of almost being somewhere and needing to get there, desperately, but . . . I'd look down—and there was nothing there.

Once you asked me when I grew up whether I wanted to marry a boy or a girl. And I said a boy. But it's not true; it was never true. I wanted girls from the earliest moments I can remember. Even when they wouldn't talk to me. When no one would talk to me. Except you. Even then I wanted girls. But I couldn't find a way to tell you. Plus I think I saw myself through your eyes—after all, only you saw something good in me, all those years. Even though you didn't really see *me*.

The Last Match

Under the bright lights of the U.S. Open semifinals, rising Russian star Sergei Sergeyev is pitted against American great Tim Porter in an epic showdown that follows two tennis titans through pivotal moments in their lives both on and off the court.

SERGEI: He cannot stop looking up at box. So I look up too. And my Galina? She is glaring at me. How could I be letting this walking injury defeat me? Many years from now, I remember that look. It will be the look I will see whenever I disappoint her. Which I will do, from time to time. Because that is what happens, in life.

For instance, last year at U.S. Open, I went through three matches like they were nothing. And then in fourth round, I play Bartok who I roomed with at the academy. He has never beaten me, but when we are playing I am remembering how he cried in his sleep for his mother, and he *tramples* me in this match. And afterwards I am so ashamed. I am walking through the hallways in daze and I do not look up. Until someone says, "You'll get him next time, Sergei." And it is Tim Porter. He says, "Your head wasn't in it." And I say, "No, my head was nowhere close to that match." And he smiles, says he can count on one hand number of matches where his head stayed in match whole time. Then he says my footwork is very fancy. And that made me happy! That Tim Porter should take any time out of his day to consider my footwork. And then he walks away. And it occurs to me that he was condescending to me. And that adds injury to insult as you say in America. And so I get frustrated. When will my life be easy?? And that night Galina has gone to bed and I am drinking with Uly, and these two ladies come up to us and they are very nice; they say how they love watching me play and I move like Canadian maple syrup what have you what have you. And I am thinking so much my life is unfair—why would Tim Porter say that about my footwork? —That when one of them puts her hand on my dick under the table—she is not shy, I guess—I let her leave it there. And when she suggests we go to her hotel room, yes I go with her. And we fuck so much. And in this time I do not *think about anything*, which feels incredible, even better than the sex we are having.

AUTHOR BIOGRAPHIES

ZAKIYYAH ALEXANDER is a stage and television writer. Her plays include *10 Things to Do Before I Die* (Second Stage Theatre), *SICK?* (New York City Summer Play Festival), *The Etymology of Bird* (Central Park SummerStage, Hip Hop Theater Festival, Providence Black Repertory Company), *Blurring Shine* (Market Theatre, Johannesburg; The New York International Fringe Festival), *Sweet Maladies* (Brava Theater Center, Rucker Theatre), and *You Are Here.* She is a recipient of a Joyce Award and Jerome Award for the development of the musical *Girl Shakes Loose Her Skin,* with composer Imani Uzuri, featuring the poetry of Sonia Sanchez. She received a MFA in Playwriting from the Yale School of Drama. She has written for *24 Legacy* and *Grey's Anatomy.*

Zakiyyah is represented by Olivier Sultan and Ally Shuster, Creative Artists Agency, 405 Lexington Avenue, 19th Floor, New York, NY 10174, 212-277-9000, olivier.sultan@caa.com, ally.shuster@caa.com.

CHRISTINA ANDERSON's plays include *The Bridgette Hobbs Connection, How to Catch Creation, Hollow Roots,* and *BlackTop Sky.* She currently teaches playwriting at SUNY Purchase College.

Christina is represented by Alexis Williams, Bret Adams Ltd, 448 W. 44th Street, New York, NY 10036, 212-765-5630, awilliams@bretadamsltd.net.

JACLYN BACKHAUS's works include *Men on Boats* (*New York Times* Critics' Pick, Clubbed Thumb), *Set in the Living Room of a Small Town American Play, Bull's Hollow, You on the Moors Now,* and the podcast *People Doing Math.* She is the 2016–17 Tow Foundation Playwright-in-Residence at Clubbed Thumb and the co-founder of Fresh Ground Pepper.

Jaclyn is represented by Derek Zasky, William Morris Endeavor Entertainment, 11 Madison Avenue, New York, NY 10010, 212-903-1396, dzasky@wmeentertainment.com.

TANYA BARFIELD's plays include: *Blue Door, Of Equal Measure, The Call,* and *Bright Half Life.* A recipient of a Lilly Award and a Helen Merrill Award, Tanya is an alumna of New Dramatists and has served on the Dramatist Guild Council. She has written for *The One Percent* (Starz) and *The Americans* (FX).

The Call (copyright © 2013) and *Bright Half Life* (copyright © 2015) are published by Dramatists Play Service, Inc. Tanya is represented by George Lane, Creative Artists Agency, 405 Lexington Avenue, 19th Floor, New York, NY 10174, 212-277-9000, glane@caa.com.

CLARE BARRON is from Wenatchee, Washington. Her plays include *You Got Older* with Page 73 Productions, directed by Anne Kauffman (Obie Award for Playwriting); *Baby Screams Miracle* (Clubbed Thumb Summerworks); *Dance Nation* (co-winner of the Relentless Award established in honor of Philip Seymour Hoffman); and *I'll Never Love Again.*

You Got Older is copyright © 2015 and is published by Samuel French, New York. Clare is represented by Rachel Viola, United Talent Agency, 888 Seventh Avenue, 9th Floor, New York, NY, 10106, 212-659-2600, violar@unitedtalent.com.

KATIE BENDER's plays include *Still Now, The Fault, One Night Only*, and *Santa Anna and Susanna*. Currently a resident artist at The New Victory Theater, her plays have been developed at The New Harmony Project, The Orchard Project, Kitchen Dog Theater, and The New Victory Theater. She is a founding member of Underbelly Theatre.

Katie is represented by Alexis Williams, Bret Adams Ltd, 448 W. 44th Street, New York, NY 10036, 212-765-5630, awilliams@bretadamsltd.net.

HILARY BETTIS's plays include: *Four People . . . , Blood & Dust, The Ghosts of Lote Bravo, The History of American Pornography, Alligator, Dakota Atoll, Mexico*, and *American Girls*. Her plays have been produced nationally and translated into Spanish. She writes for film and TV, and is a graduate of the Juilliard School.

Hilary is represented by Ally Shuster and Chris Till, Creative Artists Agency, 405 Lexington Avenue, 19th Floor, New York, NY 10174, 212-277-9000, ally.shuster@caa.com, ctill@caa.com.

JOCELYN BIOH's plays include *Nollywood Dreams, African Americans, School Girls*, and the musical *The Ladykiller's Love Story* (with music/lyrics by Cee Lo Green). As an actress, Jocelyn's New York credits include *The Curious Incident of the Dog in the Night-Time* (Broadway) and *An Octoroon* (Soho Rep.).

Jocelyn is represented by Rachel Viola, United Talent Agency, 888 Seventh Avenue, 9th Floor, New York, NY 10106, 212-500-3213, violar@unitedtalent.com.

RACHEL BONDS's plays have been developed or produced by South Coast Repertory, Ars Nova, Manhattan Theatre Club, McCarter Theatre, Roundabout Underground, Atlantic Theater Company, Studio Theatre, Actors Theatre of Louisville, SPACE on Ryder Farm, Williamstown Theatre Festival, and New York Stage & Film, among others. She is the 2016 Tow Foundation Playwright-in-Residence at Ars Nova. She received her BA at Brown University.

Rachel is represented by Olivier Sultan, Creative Artists Agency, 405 Lexington Avenue, 19th Floor, New York, NY 10174, 212-277-9000, olivier.sultan@caa.com.

JAMI BRANDLI's plays include *Technicolor Life, S.O.E., M-Theory, Sisters Three, Visiting Hours,* and *Bliss (or Emily Post Is Dead!).* Jami is the recipient of the John Gassner Memorial Playwriting Award, the Holland New Voices Award, and Aurora Theatre Company's Global Age Project Prize. She teaches at Lesley University's Low-Residency MFA program. For more information: www.jamibrandli.com.

Jami is represented by Scott Halle, Gramercy Park Entertainment, 1900 Avenue of the Stars, Suite 500, Los Angeles, CA 90067, 424-400-9747, shalle@gramercy-park.net.

BEKAH BRUNSTETTER's plays include *The Cake* (Echo Theater), *Going to a Place Where You Already Are* (South Coast Repertory), *The Oregon Trail* (O'Neill Playwrights Conference), *Be a Good Little Widow* (Ars Nova, The Old Globe), and *Oohrah!* (Atlantic Theater Company, Steppenwolf Garage). She has written for *Switched at Birth* and Starz's *American Gods,* and is a producer on NBC's *This Is Us.* Bekah received her MFA from The New School for Drama. For more information: www.bekahbrunstetter.com.

Bekah is represented by Derek Zasky, William Morris Endeavor Entertainment, 11 Madison Avenue, New York, NY 10010, 212-903-1396, dzasky@wmeentertainment.com.

SARAH BURGESS's play *Dry Powder* premiered at The Public Theater in March 2016. *Dry Powder* was a recipient of the 2016 Laurents/Hatcher Foundation Award, and a finalist for the Susan Smith Blackburn Prize. Her other plays include *Camdenside* (The Ground Floor at Berkeley Repertory Theatre) and *FAIL: Failures* (ANT Fest). She has written for *The Tenant* (Woodshed Collective) and "Naked Radio," Naked Angels's podcast series. Sarah has been a writer-in-residence at SPACE on Ryder Farm and The Cape Cod Theatre Project. She is a member of the WP Lab and is an Ars Nova Play Group alumnus.

Sarah is represented by Scott Chaloff, William Morris Endeavor Entertainment, 11 Madison Avenue, New York, NY 10010, 212-903-1503, schaloff@wmeentertainment.com.

SHEILA CALLAGHAN has received a Princess Grace Award, a Jerome Fellowship, the Susan Smith Blackburn Prize, and a Whiting Award. She's a member of the Obie-winning organization 13P and a New Dramatists alumnus. She is currently a writer/producer on Showtime's *Shameless*, and was nominated for a Golden Globe for her work on Hulu's *Casual*.

Sheila is represented by Chris Till, Creative Artists Agency, 405 Lexington Avenue, 19th Floor, New York, NY 10174, 212-277-9000, ctill@caa.com.

EUGENIE CHAN's plays include *Madame Ho, 19 Wentworth Alley, Chinatown, Kitchen Table,* and *Bone to Pick.* Her work has been performed at The Cutting Ball Theater, The San Francisco Mime Troupe, Magic Theatre, The Public Theater, Playwrights Horizons, Houston Grand Opera, among others. She's playwright emerita at The Cutting Ball Theater and an alumna of New Dramatists. www.eugeniechantheater.org.

Eugenie is represented by Toochis Morin, The Brant Rose Agency, 6671 Sunset Boulevard, Suite 1584 B, Los Angeles, CA 90028, 323-460-6464, trose@brantroseagency.com.

SAM CHANSE's work includes *Fruiting Bodies, gilgamesh & the mosquito, Delivery, about that whole dying thing, Asian American Jesus,* and *Lydia's Funeral Video.* A member of the Ma-Yi Writers Lab, Ars Nova's Play Group, and New Dramatists, she is a recent Sundance/Ucross Playwright Fellow, MacDowell Fellow, and Playwrights Realm Writing Fellow.

Sam is represented by Mark Orsini, Bret Adams Ltd, 448 W. 44th Street, New York, NY 10036, 212-765-5630, morsini@bretadamsltd.net.

MIA CHUNG's plays include *You for Me for You, Catch as Catch Can, This Exquisite Corpse,* and *Skin in the Game.* She is a member of New Dramatists, a Huntington Playwriting Fellow, and an emeritus member of the Ma-Yi Writers Lab.

You for Me for You is copyright © 2015 and is published by Bloomsbury Methuen Drama, London. Mia is represented by Antje Oegel, AO International, 540 President Street, Suite 2E, Brooklyn, NY 11215, 917-521-6640, aoegel@aoiagency.com.

ELIZA CLARK's plays include *Edgewise* (co-produced in 2010 by Page 73 Productions and The Play Company at Soho Rep.) and *Recall* (produced in 2012 by Colt Coeur at The Wild Project). *Future Thinking* had its world premiere at South Coast Repertory in April 2016.

Edgewise and *Recall* are copyright © 2014 and are published by Samuel French, New York. Eliza is represented by Derek Zasky, William Morris Endeavor Entertainment, 11 Madison Avenue, New York, NY 10010, 212-903-1396, dzasky@wmeentertainment.com.

ALEXANDRA COLLIER's plays have been developed at Sydney Theatre Company, The New Group, Women's Project Theater, New Georges, and The Lark. Her plays include *Underland* (59E59 Theaters presented by terraNOVA Collective), *Take Me Home* (a mobile theater piece taking place in a New York City taxi presented by Incubator Arts Project), and *Holy Day* (Susan Smith Blackburn Prize finalist).

Alexandra is represented by Jessica Amato, The Gersh Agency, 41 Madison Avenue, 33rd Floor, New York, NY 10010, 212-634-8119, jamato@gershny.com.

FERNANDA COPPEL is a playwright and screenwriter. Her plays include *Chimichangas and Zoloft*, *Sinaloa Cowboy*, *Pussy*, *No Homo*, and *King Liz*, among others. *King Liz* premiered at Second Stage Theatre Uptown Series in 2015, and is being developed into a TV series for *Showtime*. Fernanda is a three-year fellow at The Juilliard School, and she received her MFA from NYU.

King Liz is copyright © 2016 and is published by Samuel French, New York. Fernanda is represented by Scott Chaloff, William Morris Endeavor Entertainment, 11 Madison Avenue, New York, NY, 10010 212-903-1503, schaloff@wmeentertainment.com.

ERIN COURTNEY's plays include *I Will Be Gone*, *A Map of Virtue*, *Honey Drop*, and *Demon Baby*. She is an affiliated artist with Clubbed Thumb, a member of 13P, and she teaches playwriting at Brooklyn College. She earned her MFA in playwriting at Brooklyn College with Mac Wellman. She is a member of New Dramatists and a 2013 Guggenheim Fellow.

Erin is represented by Antje Oegel, AO International, 540 President Street, Suite 2E, Brooklyn, NY 11215, 917-521-6640, aoegel@aoiagency.com.

FRANCES YA-CHU COWHIG's plays have been produced at venues such as the National Theatre of Great Britain, Manhattan Theater Club and the Goodman Theatre. Her plays have been awarded the Wasserstein Prize, the Yale Drama Series Award, an Edinburgh Fringe First Award and the Keene Prize for Literature. Frances received a MFA in Writing from the Michener Center for Writers at UT Austin, a BA in Sociology from Brown University, and a certificate in Ensemble-Based Physical Theatre from the Dell'Arte International School of Physical Theatre. She was born in Philadelphia, and raised in Northern Virginia, Okinawa, Taipei, and Beijing. Frances is an assistant professor of drama at UC Santa Barbara.

The World of Extreme Happiness is copyright © 2014 and is published by Methuen Drama, London. Frances's commissioning editor is Anna Brewer, Methuen Drama, 50 Bedford Square, London, WC1B 3DP, +44(0)20 7 631 5684, anna. brewer@bloomsbury.com. Frances is represented by Antje Oegel, AO International, 540 President Street, Suite 2E, Brooklyn, NY 11215, 917-521-6640, aoegel@aoiagency.com.

SARAH DELAPPE's play *The Wolves* (Clubbed Thumb/Playwrights Horizons Theater School, Great Plains Theater Conference) was a recipient of the American Playwriting Foundation's inaugural Relentless Award and a Susan Smith Blackburn Prize finalist. She is affiliated with SPACE at Ryder Farm, Ars Nova Play Group, and New Georges. She received a MFA from Brooklyn College.

Sarah is represented by Di Glazer, ICM Partners, 65 E. 55th Street, New York, NY 10022, 212-556-5600, dglazer@ icmpartners.com.

LYDIA R. DIAMOND's plays include: *Smart People, Stick Fly, Voyeurs de Venus, The Bluest Eye, The Gift Horse,* and *Harriet Jacobs*. Producing theaters include: The Arden, Arena Stage, Congo Square, The Cort (Broadway), The Goodman, Hartford Stage, The Huntington, The McCarter, New Vic (Off-Broadway), Long Wharf, Playmakers Rep, Second Stage (Off-Broadway), and Steppenwolf. Lydia was a 2013–14 Playwright in Residence at Arena Stage, and a 2014–15 Radcliffe Institute Fellow.

Lydia is represented by Derek Zasky, William Morris Endeavor Entertainment, 11 Madison Avenue, New York, NY 10010, 212-903-1396, dzasky@wmeentertainment.com.

JACKIE SIBBLIES DRURY's plays include *We Are Proud to Present a Presentation About the Herero of Namibia, Formerly Known as South West Africa, From the German Sudwestafrika, Between the Years 1884–1915;* and *Social Creatures*. She has learned that long play titles beget brief playwright bios.

Jackie is represented by Antje Oegel, AO International, 540 President Street, Suite 2E, Brooklyn, NY 11215, 917-521-6640, aoegel@aoiagency.com.

LAURA EASON is a screenwriter, playwright, adaptor, and musical book writer. She's most known for her play *Sex with Strangers* (Steppenwolf, Chicago; Second Stage, New York; Geffen Playhouse, L.A.; more than twenty productions in the U.S. and internationally); and four seasons on the Emmy-nominated Netflix drama *House of Cards* (WGA nomination for outstanding writing in a drama series).

The Undeniable Sound of Right Now is copyright © 2016 and is published by Dramatists Play Service, Inc., New York. Laura is represented by Derek Zasky, William Morris Endeavor Entertainment, 11 Madison Avenue, New York, NY 10010, 212-903-1396, dzasky@wmeentertainment.com.

LARISSA FASTHORSE is an award-winning playwright, director, choreographer, and member of the Lakota Nation. She has worked with theaters across the country, such as Kansas City Rep, Perseverance Theater Company, Native Voices at the Autry, Cornerstone Theater Company, AlterTheater, Children's Theater Company of Minneapolis, and Cherokee Mountainside Theater.

Larissa is represented by Jonathan Mills, Paradigm, 360 Park Avenue South, 16th Floor, New York, NY 10010, 212-897-6400.

HALLEY FEIFFER is a playwright and actor whose plays have been produced at the Atlantic Theater Company, Manhattan Class Company, and Rattlestick Playwrights Theater, among others. They include *I'm Gonna Pray for You So Hard* and *A Funny Thing Happened on the Way to the Gynecologic Oncology Unit at Memorial Sloan-Kettering Cancer Center of New York City.*

I'm Gonna Pray for You So Hard is copyright © 2015 and is published by Overlook Press, New York. Halley is represented by Di Glazer, ICM Partners, 65 E. 55th Street, New York, NY 10022, 212-556-5600, dglazer@icmpartners.com.

LINDSEY FERRENTINO'S *Ugly Lies the Bone* was a Critic's Pick in the *New York Times* and played a sold-out, extended off-Broadway run at the Roundabout Theatre Company's Underground. She has commissions from Roundabout, The Geffen, and South Coast Repertory.

Ugly Lies the Bone is copyright © 2015 and is published by Samuel French, New York. Lindsey is represented by Chris Till, Creative Artists Agency, 405 Lexington Avenue, 19th Floor, New York, NY 10174, 212-277-9000, ctill@caa.com.

LEIGH FONDAKOWSKI was the head writer of *The Laramie Project*, an Emmy nominated co-screenwriter for the adaptation of *The Laramie Project* for HBO, and a co-writer of *The Laramie Project: Ten Years Later.* Her other original plays include: *The People's Temple, I Think I Like Girls, Spill,* and *Casa Cushman.*

Leigh is represented by Michael Moore, Michael Moore Agency, 450 W. 24th Street, Suite 1C, New York, NY 10011, 212-221-0400, michael@michaelmooreagency.com.

MADELEINE GEORGE's plays include *The (curious case of the) Watson Intelligence* (Pulitzer Prize finalist; Outer Critics Circle John Gassner Award), *Seven Homeless Mammoths Wander New England* (Susan Smith Blackburn Prize finalist), *Precious Little*, and *The Zero Hour* (Jane Chambers Award, Lambda Literary Award finalist).

The (curious case of the) Watson Intelligence is copyright © 2014 and is published by Samuel French, New York. Madeleine is represented by Seth Glewen, The Gersh Agency, 41 Madison Avenue, 33rd Floor, New York, NY 10010, 212-997-1818, sglewen@gershny.com.

SARAH GUBBINS's plays include *Fair Use, The Drinking Problem, The Kid Thing* (Jeff Award, Edgerton Foundation New American Play Award), *fml: how Carson McCullers saved my life*, and *Cocked*. Sarah is a Core Writer of the Playwrights' Center, a former Carl J. Djerassi Fellow and Jerome Fellow. She holds a MFA from Northwestern University. She lives in Los Angeles.

Sarah is represented by Mark Subias, United Talent Agency, 888 Seventh Avenue, 7th Floor, New York, NY 10106, 212-659-2615, subiasm@unitedtalent.com.

DIPIKA GUHA was born in India and raised in tea-drinking countries. Her plays include *Mechanics of Love, The Art of Gaman*, and *The Rules*. Dipika has a MFA in Playwriting from the Yale School of Drama, where she studied under Paula Vogel. She is currently a Visiting Artist at the Schell Center for International Human Rights at Yale University. She is under commission from Oregon Shakespeare Festival and South Coast Repertory. For more information: www.dipikaguha.com.

Dipika is represented by Mark Orsini and Bruce Ostler, Bret Adams Ltd, 448 W. 44th Street, New York, NY 10036, 212-765-5630, morsini@bretadamsltd.net, bostler@bretadamsltd.net.

KAREN HARTMAN's plays include *Roz and Ray, The Book of Joseph, Project Dawn, Gum, Leah's Train, Going Gone, Girl Under Grain, Wild Kate, ALICE: Tales of a Curious Girl* (Music by Gina

Leishman), and *Troy Women*. Her work has been published by Theatre Communications Group, Dramatists Play Service, Playscripts, Backstage Books, and NoPassport. She held the Playwrights' Center's McKnight Residency and Commission in 2014–15, and is an alumna of New Dramatists. She has won awards from the Rockefeller Foundation at Bellagio, the NEA, the Helen Merrill Foundation, and the Jerome Foundation. She was a Hodder Fellow at Princeton University, and a Fulbright scholar. Her prose has been published in the *New York Times* and *Washington Post*.

Karen is represented by Di Glazer, ICM Partners, 65 E. 55th Street, New York, NY 10022, 212-556-5600, dglazer@icmpartners.com.

AMINA HENRY is a playwright whose work has been developed and produced at The New Group, Clubbed Thumb, P73, The Flea, National Black Theater, Dixon Place, The Cell, Theater for the New City, Barefoot Theatre, JACK, Drama of Works, The Brick, Oregon Shakespeare Festival, Kitchen Dog Theater, Cohesion Theatre Company, Brooklyn College, and Texas State University. She is a graduate of the MFA Playwriting program at Brooklyn College.

Amina is represented by Max Grossman, Abrams Artists Agency, 275 Seventh Avenue, 26th Floor, New York, NY 10001, 646-461-9372, mgrossman@abramsartny.com.

LAURA JACQMIN's plays include *Residence* (Actors Theatre of Louisville's 40th Humana Festival of New Plays), *January Joiner* (Long Wharf Theatre), *Ski Dubai* (Steppenwolf Theatre), *Dental Society Midwinter Meeting* (Chicago Dramatists/At Play, 16th Street Theater, Williamstown Theatre Festival), *A Third* (Finborough), and *Look, We Are Breathing* (Rivendell Theatre). For TV, Laura has written for *Grace and Frankie* and *Lucky 7*. She worked on the videogames *Minecraft: Story Mode* and *The Walking Dead—A New Frontier: The Telltale Series*. Her awards include the Wasserstein Prize, two NEA Art Works grants, the Kennedy Center David Mark Cohen Award, and two MacDowell fellowships.

Laura is represented by Derek Zasky, William Morris Endeavor Entertainment, 11 Madison Avenue, New York, NY 10010, 212-903-1396, dzasky@wmeentertainment.com.

HANSOL JUNG's plays include *Cardboard Piano, No More Sad Things, Wolf Play, Among the Dead,* and *Wild Goose Dreams.* She has translated more than thirty English musicals into Korean, including *Evita, Dracula,* and *Spamalot,* while working on several award-winning productions as director, lyricist, and translator in Seoul. Hansol is a proud member of the Ma-Yi Writers Lab.

Hansol is represented by Ben Izzo, Abrams Artists Agency, 275 Seventh Avenue, 26th Floor, New York, NY 10001, 646-461-9383, ben.izzo@abramsartny.com.

MJ KAUFMAN's work has been seen at the Huntington Theatre, New York Theatre Workshop, Yale School of Drama, the New Museum, Clubbed Thumb, New Georges, P73, Colt Coeur, Aurora Theater, Crowded Fire, New Harmony Project, Playwrights Foundation, Young Playwrights Inc., and performed in Russian in Moscow. MJ received the 2013 ASCAP Cole Porter Prize in Playwriting, the 2013 Global Age Project Prize, and the 2010 Jane Chambers Prize in Feminist Theatre. MJ is a Huntington Theater Playwriting Fellow, Colt Coeur member, InterAct Theatre Core Playwright, and a member of the 2018 Public Theater Emerging Writers' Group. MJ has a MFA from the Yale School of Drama.

MJ is represented by Beth Blickers, APA, 135 W. 50th Street, 17th Floor, New York, NY 10020, 212-245-5062, bblickers@apa-agency.com.

NAMBI E. KELLEY has written plays for Steppenwolf, the Goodman Theatre, the Court Theatre, the American Blues Theater, and Lincoln Center, among others. Kelley is playwright-in-residence at the National Black Theatre in New York and is currently working on an adaptation of Toni Morrison's *Jazz.* For more information: www.nambikelley.com.

Native Son is copyright © 2016 and is published by Samuel French, New York. Nambi is represented by Leah Hamos,

The Gersh Agency, 41 Madison Ave, 33rd Floor, New York, NY 10010, 212-634-8153, lhamos@gersh.com.

GEORGETTE KELLY is an award-winning playwright, translator, and educator. Her plays include *Ballast, F*ck la vie d'artiste, In the Belly of the Whale, how to hero or the subway play, I Carry Your Heart*, and an adaptation of Jeanette Winterson's novel *Lighthousekeeping*. For more information: georgettekelly.com.

Georgette is represented by Amy Wagner, Abrams Artists Agency, 275 Seventh Avenue, 26th Floor, New York, NY 10001, 646-486-4600, amy.wagner@abramsartny.com.

BOO KILLEBREW is a playwright, actress, and co-founder of CollaborationTown Theatre Company. Boo is a Lila Acheson Playwriting Fellow at The Juilliard School, and the recipient of The Vineyard Theatre's Paula Vogel Playwriting Award. She is an alumna of the Emerging Writers Group at The Public Theater, a resident of SPACE's The Working Farm, a recipient of a NYFA Fellowship, an alumna of TerraNova's Groundbreakers, and an Affiliated Artist and Kitchen Cabinet Member with New Georges. She is a writer for *Longmire* (A&E, Netflix) and created the television pilot, *Aim High* (The Sundance Channel).

Boo is represented by Rachel Viola, United Talent Agency, 888 Seventh Avenue, 9th Floor, New York, NY, 10106, 212-659-2600, violar@unitedtalent.com.

BASIL KREIMENDAHL is a resident playwright at New Dramatists. Basil's plays have been developed or produced by Actors Theater of Louisville, The O'Neill, New York Theatre Workshop, American Theater Company, Victory Gardens, Rattlestick Theater, and The Oregon Shakespeare Festival, among others. Basil was awarded a Jerome and a McKnight Fellowship, and received an Arts Meets Activism grant for work with the trans community. Basil received a MFA from University of Iowa in 2013.

Basil is represented by Beth Blickers, APA, 135 W. 50th Street, 17th Floor, New York, NY 10020, 212-245-5062, bblickers@apa-agency.com.

KIMBER LEE's plays include *to the yellow house, tokyo fish story*, and *brownsville song (b-side for tray)*. Kimber has received productions at Actors Theatre of Louisville, LCT3, Long Wharf, Center Theatre Group, South Coast Repertory, and Philadelphia Theatre Company, among others. She is the recipient of the Ruby Prize, a PoNY Fellowship, the New Voices Fellowship/Hartford Stage Award, a PoNY/Bush Theatre Playwright Residency (London), and she is a member of the Ma-Yi Writers Lab. Kimber received a MFA from UT Austin.

Kimber is represented by Seth Glewen, The Gersh Agency, 41 Madison Avenue, 33rd Floor, New York, NY 10010, 212-997-1818, sglewen@gershny.com.

MARTYNA MAJOK's plays have been presented at Steppenwolf Theatre Company, Williamstown Theatre Festival, Rattlestick Playwrights Theatre, and Actors Theatre of Louisville. Awards include The David Calicchio Emerging American Playwright Prize, New York Theatre Workshop's 2050 Fellowship, Global Age Project Prize, and the 2015–16 PoNY Fellowship at the Lark Play Development Center.

Martyna is represented by Olivier Sultan, Creative Artists Agency, 405 Lexington Avenue, 19th Floor, New York, NY 10174, 212-277-9000, olivier.sultan@caa.com.

MONA MANSOUR's plays include *Unseen*, *The Way West* (Steppenwolf, Labyrinth Theater), *The Vagrant* (Sundance Theater Institute), *The Hour of Feeling* (Humana, High Tide Festival), *Urge for Going* (The Public Theater, Golden Thread), and *Falling Down the Stairs*, with Tala Manassah, an EST/Sloan commission about a scientist in 1970s Iraq. With Tala she wrote "Dressing," part of *Facing Our Truth: Short Plays on Trayvon, Race and Privilege*, commissioned by the New Black Fest. Mona was awarded the 2012 Whiting Award and the 2014 Middle East America Playwright Award. For more information: monamansour.com.

Mona is represented by Jessica Amato, The Gersh Agency, 41 Madison Avenue, 33rd Floor, New York, NY 10010, 212-634-8119, jamato@gershny.com.

MEG MIROSHNIK's plays include *The Fairytale Lives of Russian Girls* (Yale Rep, Alliance), *The Droll* (Undermain, Pacific Playwrights Festival), *The Tall Girls* (Alliance, O'Neill, La Jolla DNA Festival), and *Lady Tattoo* (Pacific Playwrights Festival, Rattlestick F*cking Good Plays Festival). Meg received the Whiting Award, an Alliance/Kendeda Graduate Playwriting Award, and was a Susan Smith Blackburn Prize finalist. She has commissions from South Coast Repertory, Steppenwolf, and Yale Rep. Meg is a Core Writer at the Playwrights' Center. She received her MFA from the Yale School of Drama. She is a founding member of The Kilroys.

The Tall Girls is copyright © 2014 and is published by Samuel French, New York. Meg is represented by Jonathan Lomma, William Morris Endeavor Entertainment, 11 Madison Avenue, New York, NY 10010, 212-903-1552, jlomma@ wmeentertainment.com.

REHANA LEW MIRZA's productions include *Soldier X* (Ma-Yi, Kilroy's selection, NYSCA Commission), *Lonely Leela* (LPAC), and *Barriers* (Desipina, AATC). Rehana's awards include an NNPN commission via InterAct, an IAAC/Lark residency, a TCG/New Georges fellowship, a Tofte Lake residency, and an EST/Sloan commission. Rehana is affiliated with Ma-Yi Writers Lab and Primary Stages' Dorothy Strelsin Writers Group. She received a MFA from Columbia University and a BFA from NYU's Tisch School of the Arts.

Rehana is represented by Leah Hamos, The Gersh Agency, 41 Madison Avenue, 33rd Floor, New York, NY 10010, 212-634-8153, lhamos@gersh.com.

ANNA MOENCH's awards include the Kennedy Center's Paul Stephen Lim Playwriting Award, the NYFA Fellowship, the Jerome Fellowship, the Van Lier Fellowship, East West Players' 2042 Competition, the Jerome Travel Grant, and two EST/Sloan commissions. Anna is an alumna of EST's Youngblood and The Public's Emerging Writers Group, and is currently an MFA candidate at UCSD. For more information: www.annamoench.com.

Anna is represented by Ally Shuster, Creative Artists Agency, 405 Lexington Avenue, 19th Floor, New York, NY 10174, 212-277-9000, ally.shuster@caa.com.

DOMINIQUE MORISSEAU's plays include *Skeleton Crew* (Atlantic Theatre Company), *Paradise Blue* (Williamstown), *Detroit '67* (The Public Theater, Classical Theatre of Harlem), *Sunset Baby* (LAByrinth), *Follow Me to Nellie's* (O'Neill, Premiere Stages), and *Pipeline* (Lincoln Center Theater). Dominique has received the Weissberger Award, the Stavis Award, a PoNY Fellowship, the Steinberg Award, and the Edward M. Kennedy Prize for Drama. Her trilogy, *The Detroit Project*, is forthcoming from Theatre Communications Group.

Skeleton Crew is copyright © 2015 and is published by Samuel French, New York. Dominique is represented by Jonathan Mills, Paradigm Agency, 360 Park Avenue South, 16th Floor, New York, NY 10010, 212-897-6400, jmills@paradigmagency.com.

JULIE MARIE MYATT's play, *The Happy Ones*, premiered at South Coast Repertory, and won the LA Drama Critic Circle's Ted Schmitt Award for Outstanding New Play. *Welcome Home, Jenny Sutter* premiered at Oregon Shakespeare Festival, and a tour of that production went to the Kennedy Center as part of the Kennedy Center Fund for New American Plays. Her play, *Someday*, premiered as part of Cornerstone Theater's Justice Cycle. She received a Walt Disney Studios Screenwriting Fellowship, a Jerome Fellowship at The Playwrights' Center, and a McKnight Advancement Grant. She is currently working on commissions for Roundabout Theatre, Yale Rep, and Center Theatre Group. She is an ensemble member of Cornerstone Theater Company and an alumna of New Dramatists.

Julie is represented by Bruce Ostler and Mark Orsini, Bret Adams Ltd, 448 W. 44th Street, New York, NY 10036, 212-765-5630, bostler@bretadamsltd.net, morsini@bretadamsltd.net.

JANINE NABERS's plays include *Annie Bosh Is Missing* (Steppenwolf Theatre Company, 2013), *Serial Black Face* (winner of the 2014 Yale Drama Prize*)*, *A Swell in the Ground*, *Welcome to Jesus*

(Hartford Stage), and the Ted Hughes/Sylvia Plath musical *Mrs. Hughes*. She is currently working on commissions from Primary Stages and the Alley Theater. Janine divides her time between Los Angeles and New York City where she currently writes for TV and film.

Janine is represented by Scott Chaloff, William Morris Endeavor Entertainment, 11 Madison Avenue, New York, NY 10010, 212-903-1503, schaloff@wmeentertainment.com.

MARY KATHRYN NAGLE is a citizen of the Cherokee Nation. She is a playwright and attorney. Her work focuses on the restoration of the inherent sovereignty of Tribal Nations, including her own Cherokee Nation. Her plays include *Manahatta*, *Miss Lead*, and *Fairly Traceable*. She has been commissioned by Arena Stage, Portland Center Stage, and The Rose Theater.

Mary is represented by Michael Finkle, William Morris Endeavor Entertainment, 11 Madison Avenue, New York, NY 10010, 212-903-1144, mfinkle@wmeentertainment.com.

LYNN NOTTAGE is the first woman to be awarded the Pulitzer Prize for Drama twice—for *Ruined* and *Sweat*. Her plays have been produced widely in the U.S. and throughout the world. They include *Sweat*; *By the Way, Meet Vera Stark* (Lily Award, Drama Desk nomination); *Ruined* (Pulitzer Prize, Obie, Lucille Lortel, New York Drama Critics' Circle, Audelco, Drama Desk, and Outer Critics Circle Awards); *Intimate Apparel* (American Theatre Critics and New York Drama Critics' Circle Awards for Best Play); *Fabulation, or The Re-Education of Undine* (Obie Award); *Crumbs from the Table of Joy*; *Las Meninas*; *Mud, River, Stone*; *Por'knockers*; and *POOF!* Lynn is the recipient of a MacArthur "Genius" Fellowship, the Steinberg "Mimi" Distinguished Playwright Award, the Dramatists Guild Hull-Warriner Award, the inaugural Horton Foote Prize, the Lilly Award, the Helen Hayes Award, the Lee Reynolds Award, and the Jewish World Watch iWitness Award.

Lynn is represented by Olivier Sultan, Creative Artists Agency, 405 Lexington Avenue, 19th Floor, New York, NY 10174, 212-277-9000, olivier.sultan@caa.com.

JIEHAE PARK's plays include *peerless* (Yale Rep, CL Mentor Project) and *Hannah and the Dread Gazebo*. She is one of the writers of *Wondrous Strange* (Humana). Jihae's work has been developed by Soho Rep., Playwrights Horizons, Berkeley Rep, The Public Theater, New York Theatre Workshop, Old Globe, DG, Ojai, BAPF, and Ma-Yi. Jihae is a Hodder fellow, and is the recipient of the Leah Ryan Award, the Princess Grace Award, a Weissberger Award, and a winner of the Ashland New Plays Festival's Women's Invitational. Jihae has commissions from Playwrights Horizons, the McCarter Theatre Center, and Williamstown, and is a member of New Dramatists.

Jihae is represented by Michael Finkle, William Morris Endeavor Entertainment, 11 Madison Avenue, New York, NY 10010, 212-903-1144, mfinkle@wmeentertainment.com.

LISA RAMIREZ's plays include *Exit Cuckoo (nanny in motherland)* (first presented Off-Broadway by the Working Theater, Colman Domingo, director); *Art of Memory* (Company SoGoNo commission, presented at the 3-Legged Dog, New York, Tanya Calamoneri, director); *Pas de Deux (lost my shoe)* (Cherry Lane Mentor Project 15, New York, Cynthia Hopkins, mentor); *To the Bone* (commissioned by Working Theater, Mark Plesant, director; Cherry Lane Theatre, Lisa Peterson, director); and *All Fall Down* (conceived at INTAR during the Maria Irene Fornés Hispanic Playwrights in Residency Lab). Lisa is a proud recipient of the 2015 NYCT Helen Merrill Emerging Playwriting Award and honored to be on the 2015 Kilroy List!

Lisa is represented by Gloria Bonelli and Associates, 11 Victoria Terrace, Goshen, NY 10924, 646-498-3607, glo@gloriabonelli.com.

THERESA'S REBECK's plays have been widely produced nationally and internationally. She is the creator of the television series *Smash*. Her third novel, *I'm Glad about You*, was published by Putnam in 2016.

Theresa is represented by ICM Partners, 65 E. 55th Street, New York, NY 10022, 212-556-5600.

GABRIELLE REISMAN is a founder/director of the immersive theater company Underbelly. She's a playwright-in-residence for the NOLA Project, with whom she originally developed *Catch the Wall*. She's developed work with Sundance, the MacDowell Colony, and Page73, among others. Her plays have been produced throughout the U.S. and translated into German. For more information: gabriellereisman.com.

Gabrielle is represented by Alexis Williams, Bret Adams Ltd, 448 W. 44th Street, New York, NY 10036, 212-765-5630, awilliams@bretadamsltd.net.

AMELIA ROPER has been commissioned by Yale Rep, Oregon Shakespeare Festival, Marin Theatre Company, Colt Coeur, and The Rose. Her plays have been produced at the Humana Festival, Crowded Fire, and developed at Soho Rep., Berkeley Repertory Theater, the Old Vic, and the Melbourne Theatre Company. Amelia received her MFA from the Yale School of Drama.

Amelia is represented by Jonathan Mills, Paradigm Agency, 360 Park Avenue South, 16th Floor, New York, NY 10010, 212-897-6400, jmills@paradigmagency.com.

MELISSA ROSS's play *Thinner Than Water* is included in *New Playwrights: Best Plays of 2011*. Her plays *Of Good Stock* and *Nice Girl* each received 2015 productions at South Coast Repertory, Manhattan Theater Club, and Labyrinth Theater Company. She is a graduate of the Juilliard School.

Of Good Stock is licensed and published by Dramatists Play Service, Inc., New York. Melissa is represented by Jessica Amato, The Gersh Agency, 41 Madison Avenue, 33rd Floor, New York, NY 10010, 212-634-8119, jamato@gershny.com.

SHARYN ROTHSTEIN is a playwright and television writer. Her plays include *By The Water* (recipient of the 2015 Francesca Primus Prize), *All The Days* (McCarter Theatre Center, May 2016), among others. Sharyn has a MFA from NYU, and is a proud and grateful alumna of many of New York's best emerging writer groups.

Sharyn is represented by Di Glazer, ICM Partners, 65 E. 55th Street, New York, NY 10022, 212-556-5600, dglazer@ icmpartners.com.

TANYA SARACHO was born in Los Mochis, Sinaloa, México. She is a playwright who writes for TV (*How to Get Away with Murder*, HBO's *Looking* and *Girls*, and *Devious Maids*). She is the creator and showrunner for *Pour Vida*, (Starz, in development). She was named Best New Playwright by *Chicago Magazine*. Tanya's plays have been produced at Primary Stages, Second Stage, Denver Theatre Center, Oregon Shakespeare Festival, The Goodman Theater, Steppenwolf Theatre, Teatro Vista, Teatro Luna, Fountain Theatre, Clubbed Thumb, NEXT Theatre, and 16th Street Theater. Tanya was named one of nine national Latino "Luminarios" by *Café* magazine and given the first Revolucionario Award in Theater by the National Museum of Mexican Art. She is the founder of Teatro Luna (the first all-Latina theater company in the nation) and of ALTA (Alliance of Latino Theatre Artists). She is currently in development with Big Beach Films for a project about brujería, and has commissions from South Coast Repertory and Two Rivers Theater.

Tanya is represented by Mark Orsini, Bret Adams Ltd, 448 W. 44th Street, New York, NY 10036, 212-765-5630, morsini@ bretadamsltd.net.

LAURA SCHELLHARDT's plays include *Ever in the Glades*, *The Comparables*, *Upright Grand*, *Air Guitar High*, *Auctioning the Ainsleys*, *The K of D*, *Courting Vampires*, and *Shapeshifter*. Adaptations include *The Phantom Tollbooth* and *The Outfit*. She is also the author of *Screenwriting for Dummies*. Laura currently heads the undergraduate playwriting program at Northwestern University and is a Victory Gardens ensemble playwright.

Laura is represented by Seth Glewen, The Gersh Agency, 41 Madison Avenue, 33rd Floor, New York, NY 10010, 212-997-1818, sglewen@gershny.com.

HEIDI SCHRECK is a playwright and actor living in Brooklyn. Her most recent play, *Grand Concourse*, received a 2015 Lilly Award, and was a finalist for the Susan Smith Blackburn Prize. Other plays include *There Are No More Big Secrets*, produced by Rattlestick (*Time Out New York* and *New York Magazine* critic's picks); *The Consultant* (Long Wharf, 2014), and *Creature*, presented by Page 73 and New Georges. Heidi has received two Obies, a Drama Desk, and the Theatre World Award.

Heidi's plays are published by Samuel French, New York. She is represented by Di Glazer, ICM Partners, 65 E. 55th Street, New York, NY 10022, 212-556-5600, dglazer@icmpartners.com.

JENNY SCHWARTZ's plays include *Iowa*, *God's Ear*, *Somewhere Fun*, *41-derful*, and *Cause for Alarm*. With Todd Almond, she received the Frederick Loewe Award for the development of *Iowa*. *Iowa* was also nominated for Lucille Lortel and Drama League Awards. Other awards include the American Academy of Arts and Letters' Benjamin H. Danks Award, a Kesselring honor, two grants from Lincoln Center's Lecomte Du Nuoy Foundation, two residencies with the Sundance Theatre Institute, and Soho Rep.'s Dorothy Strelsin Fellowship. Jenny is a two-time Susan Smith Blackburn Prize finalist, and an alumna of Juilliard and New Dramatists.

Somewhere Fun is copyright @ 2014 and is published by Samuel French, New York. Jenny is represented by Rachel Viola, United Talent Agency, 888 Seventh Avenue, 9th Floor, New York, NY 10106, 212-659-2600, violar@unitedtalent.com.

JEN SILVERMAN's plays include *The Roommate* (Actor's Theatre of Louisville, Humana, 2015); *Wondrous Strange* (Humana, 2016); *The Moors* (Yale Rep); *The Dangerous House of Pretty Mbane* (InterAct Theatre, Barrymore Award); *Crane Story* (Playwrights Realm); and *Phoebe in Winter* (Clubbed Thumb). She has developed plays as workshop productions: *The Hunters* (Cherry Lane Mentor Project, Lynn Nottage, mentor); *Wild Blue* and *Still* (Juilliard); and *That Poor Girl and How He Killed Her* (Playwrights Horizons Theatre School, commission). She is a member of New Dramatists, a Core Writer at the Playwrights' Center in Minneapolis, and has developed work at the O'Neill, PlayPenn, SPACE on Ryder Farm, Williamstown, New York Theatre Workshop, and the Royal Court in London, among others. She's a two-time MacDowell fellow, and a recipient of the Kennedy Center's Paula Vogel Playwriting Award, a New York Foundation for the Arts grant, a Leah Ryan Fellowship/ Lilly Award, the 2015 Helen Merrill Fund Award for emerging playwrights, and the Yale Drama Series Award for *Still*. Jen received degrees at Brown, Iowa Playwrights Workshop, and Juilliard. For more information: www.jensilverman.com.

Jen is represented by Rachel Viola, United Talent Agency, 888 Seventh Avenue, 9th Floor, New York, NY 10106, 212-659-2600, violar@unitedtalent.com.

CHARISE CASTRO SMITH is a playwright, television writer, and actor from Miami. Playwriting credits include *Feathers and Teeth* (Goodman Theater); *Estrella Cruz (The Junkyard Queen)* (Ars Nova, Halycon Theatre); *The Hunchback of Seville* (Washington Ensemble Theater, Trinity Rep); *Washeteria* (Soho Rep.); and *Boomcracklefly* (Miracle Theater). Charise has a MFA from the Yale School of Drama.

Charise is represented by Di Glazer, ICM Partners, 65 E. 55th Street, New York, NY 10022, 212-556-5600, dglazer@icmpartners.com.

RUBY RAE SPIEGEL's *Dry Land* premiered Off-Broadway in 2014 at Colt Coeur, following development at New York Stage and Film's Powerhouse Theater Readings Festival and the Ojai Playwrights Conference. A finalist for the Susan Smith Blackburn Prize, the play been produced throughout the U.S. and in London. Ruby's play *Carrie & Francine* premiered in the Summer Shorts Festival in 2011 at 59E59 alongside work by Neil LaBute and Christopher Durang. Ruby currently writes for Netflix's original series *The OA*. She is a 2015 graduate of Yale University.

Dry Land is copyright © 2015 and is published by Dramatists Play Service, Inc. Ruby is represented by Scott Chaloff,

William Morris Endeavor Entertainment, 11 Madison Avenue, New York, NY 10010, 212-903-1503, schaloff@wmeentertainment.com.

SUSAN SOON HE STANTON's plays include *Takarazuka!!!*, *SEEK*, *Cygnus*, *The Things Are Against Us*, and *Today Is My Birthday*. She was the inaugural recipient of the Van Lier Playwriting Fellowship at the Lark and received a feature film development grant from the Sloan Foundation. Raised in Honolulu, Susan now lives in New York City.

Susan is represented by Jessica Amato, The Gersh Agency, 41 Madison Avenue, 33rd Floor, New York, NY 10010, 212-634-8119, jamato@gershny.com.

KATE TARKER's plays include *Thunderbodies*, *An Almanac for Farmers and Lovers in Mexico*, and *Laura and the Sea* (finalist, L. Arnold Weissberger Award). Kate is a member of Ars Nova Play Group and a Core Writer of Playwrights' Center. She has a commission from The Wilma Theater and is the recipient of a Theater Masters Visionary Playwright Award. Kate received her BA from Reed College and her MFA from the Yale School of Drama.

Kate is represented by Ross Weiner, ICM Partners, 65 E. 55th Street, New York, NY 10022, 212-556-5600, rweiner@icmpartners.com.

STEPHANIE TIMM's play *Tails of Wasps* was nominated for the Susan Smith Blackburn Prize and premiered at New Century Theatre Company. She received an Elizabeth George Commission from South Coast Repertory. She adapted *The Ramayana* for ACT Theatre's 2012 mainstage season, with playwright Yussef el Guindi. Her play *Sweet Nothing: A Grim (Fairy)Tale*, produced by Macha Monkey, was nominated for a Gregory Award in 2012 for Best New Play. Her play *On the Nature of Dust*, produced by New Century Theatre Company, developed by Portland Center Stage and Icicle Creek/ACT, was nominated for a Gregory Award in 2010 for Best New Play. Her plays have also been produced and developed at Theatre B, Washington Ensemble Theatre, Elements Theatre Collective,

Barnyard Theatre, Looking Glass Theatre, Live Girls Theatre, and Boots Up Theatre Company, among others.

Stephanie is represented by Mark Orsini, Bret Adams Ltd, 448 W. 44th Street, New York, NY 10036, 212-765-5630, morsini@bretadamsltd.net.

MFONISO UDOFIA's plays include *Sojourners* (Edgerton New Play Award, produced by Playwrights Realm and the Magic Theatre); *runboyrun* (Edgerton New Play Award, produced by the Magic Theatre), *The Grove, Her Portmanteau*, and *In Old Age*. Mfoniso is an artist and educator based in New York City.

Mfoniso is represented by Leah Hamos, The Gersh Agency, 41 Madison Avenue, 33rd Floor, New York, NY 10010, 212-634-8153, lhamos@gersh.com.

PAULA VOGEL's plays include *How I Learned to Drive* (winner of the Pulitzer Prize, Obie, Drama Desk and New York Drama Critics Circle Awards), *Indecent, The Long Christmas Ride Home, The Civil War Christmas*, and *The Baltimore Waltz*. Paula has had a distinguished career as a teacher and mentor to younger playwrights, first at Brown University and most recently at the Yale School of Drama.

Paula is represented by Jonathan Lomma, William Morris Endeavor Entertainment, 11 Madison Avenue, New York, NY, 10010, 212-903-1552, jlomma@wmeentertainment.com.

KATHRYN WALAT's plays include *Romeo & Naomi Ramirez* (2015 Kilroys List, developed at the Playwrights' Center); *See Bat Fly* (2014 Kilroys List, workshop production at Brown/Trinity Playwrights Rep); *Creation* (Theatre @ Boston Court, Ovation Award for Playwriting nomination); *Bleeding Kansas* (Hangar Theatre, Francesca Primus Award citation); and *Victoria Martin: Math Team Queen* (Women's Project, published in *New Playwrights: The Best Plays of 2007*). For more information: www.kathrynwalat.com.

Kathryn is represented by Seth Glewen, The Gersh Agency, 41 Madison Avenue, 33rd Floor, New York, NY 10010, 212-997-1818, sglewen@gershny.com.

TIMBERLAKE WERTENBAKER's plays include *The Grace of Mary Traverse, The Love of the Nightingale, Our Country's Good, The Ash Girl, Galileo's Daughter, Our Ajax,* and *The Ant and the Cicada*. She has received numerous awards, including the Olivier and the New York Drama Critics' Award for *Our Country's Good*, the Critics' Circle Award and the Susan Smith Blackburn Prize for *Three Birds Alighting on a Field*, and the 2016 Writers Guild of Great Britain Award for *Jefferson's Garden*.

Jefferson's Garden is copyright © 2015 and is published by Faber & Faber, London. Timberlake is represented by Julia Kreitman, The Agency, 24 Pottery Lane, Holland Park, London W11 4LZ, +44 (0)20-7727-1346, jk-office@theagency.co.uk.

CALAMITY WEST is an award-winning playwright. Her Kilroys-cited play, *Give It All Back*, was developed at Sideshow Theatre and Victory Gardens in 2015. Her full-length plays include *Rolling, Ibsen Is Dead!, The Peacock, The Gacy Play,* and *Common Hatred*.

Calamity is represented by Leah Hamos, The Gersh Agency, 41 Madison Avenue, 33rd Floor, New York, NY 10010, 212-634-8153, lhamos@gersh.com.

LEAH NANAKO WINKLER's plays include *Kentucky* (Page 73 and Youngblood/EST), *Death for Sydney Black* (terraNova Collective), and *Double Suicide at Ueno Park!!!* (35th Marathon of One-Act Plays). She is a current member of Youngblood and the Dorothy Strelsin New American Writers Group at Primary Stages. For more information: www.leahwinkler.org.

Kentucky is copyright © 2016 and is published by Dramatists Play Service, Inc. Leah is represented by Beth Blickers, APA, 135 W. 50th Street, 17th Floor, New York, NY 10020, 212-245-5062, bblickers@apa-agency.com.

BESS WOHL's plays include *Small Mouth Sounds, American Hero, Barcelona, Touched* and *In*. They have been produced at theaters in New York and throughout the country. She won a special Drama Desk Award for "establishing herself as an important voice in New York theater." She is a graduate of Harvard and the Yale School of Drama.

Bess is represented by Chris Till, Creative Artists Agency, 405 Lexington Avenue, 19th Floor, New York, NY 10174, 212-277-9000, ctill@caa.com.

LAUREN YEE's plays include *Ching Chong Chinaman* (Pan Asian, Mu Performing Arts, SIS Productions, Impact), *The Hatmaker's Wife* (Playwrights Realm, The Hub, Moxie, AlterTheater), *Hookman* (Encore, Company One), *In a Word* (SF Playhouse, Cleveland Public, Strawdog), *King of the Yees* (Goodman New Stages), *Samsara* (Victory Gardens, Chance, O'Neill), and *The Tiger Among Us* (MAP Fund, Mu). Lauren received her BA from Yale and her MFA from UCSD. For more information: www.laurenyee.com.

Lauren is represented by Antje Oegel, AO International, 540 President Street, Suite 2E, Brooklyn, NY, 11215, 917-521-6640, aoegel@aoiagency.com.

STEFANIE ZADRAVEC is a New Dramatists resident. Her plays include *The Electric Baby* (Two River Theater, Quantum), *Honey Brown Eyes* (Theater J, Working Theater, SF Playhouse), and *Colony Collapse* (Theatre @ Boston Court). Stefanie's honors include the Helen Merrill Award, the Primus Prize, the Helen Hayes Award, the Sustainable Arts Foundation Award, and support from NYFA, The Lark, Playwrights Realm, Dramatists Guild, the NEA, Mellon, Edgerton, Ford Foundation, and NYSCA. Stefanie's plays have been developed at Oregon Shakespeare Festival, PlayPenn, Epic Theatre, and Ryder Farm. For more information: www.szadravec.com.

Stefanie's plays are published by Dramatists Play Service, Inc., and included in *Best Women's Stage Monologues* (Smith & Kraus).

ANNA ZIEGLER's plays include *Photograph 51* (directed by Michael Grandage and starring Nicole Kidman, London, 2015), *A Delicate Ship*, and *Another Way Home*. Residencies include Sundance Theatre Lab, O'Neill National Playwrights

Conference, Williamstown Theatre Festival, New York Stage and Film, Cape Cod Theatre Project, Soho Rep.'s Writer/Director Lab, and many more.

Anna is represented by Seth Glewen, The Gersh Agency, 41 Madison Avenue, 33rd Floor, New York, NY 10010, 212-997-1818, sglewen@gershny.com.

THE KILROYS

FOUNDER BIOGRAPHIES

ZAKIYYAH ALEXANDER is a stage and television writer. Her plays include *10 Things to Do Before I Die* (Second Stage Theatre), *SICK?* (New York City Summer Play Festival), *The Etymology of Bird* (Central Park SummerStage, Hip Hop Theater Festival, Providence Black Repertory Company), *Blurring Shine* (Market Theatre, Johannesburg; The New York International Fringe Festival), *Sweet Maladies* (Brava Theater Center, Rucker Theatre), and *You Are Here*. She is a recipient of a Joyce Award and Jerome Award for the development of the musical *Girl Shakes Loose Her Skin,* with composer Imani Uzuri, featuring the poetry of Sonia Sanchez. She received a MFA in Playwriting from the Yale School of Drama. She has written for *24 Legacy* and *Grey's Anatomy*.

BEKAH BRUNSTETTER's plays include *The Cake* (Echo Theater), *Going to a Place Where You Already Are* (South Coast Repertory), *The Oregon Trail* (O'Neill Playwright's Conference), *Be a Good Little Widow* (Ars Nova, The Old Globe), and *Oohrah!* (Atlantic Theater Company; Steppenwolf Garage). She has written for *Switched at Birth* and Starz's *American Gods*, and is a producer on NBC's *This Is Us*. Bekah received her MFA from The New School for Drama. For more information: www.bekah-brunstetter.com.

SHEILA CALLAGHAN has received a Princess Grace Award, a Jerome Fellowship, the Susan Smith Blackburn Prize, and a Whiting Award. She's a member of the Obie-winning organization 13P and a New Dramatists alumnus. She is currently a writer/producer on Showtime's *Shameless*, and was nominated for a Golden Globe for her work on Hulu's *Casual*.

CARLA CHING is a native Angeleno who fell into theater in New York. Her plays include *Nomad Motel* (City Theatre, O'Neill Playwrights Conference), *The Two Kids That Blow Shit Up* (Artists at Play, Mu Performing Arts, Huntington's Breaking Ground Festival), *Fast Company* (EST, South Coast Repertory, Lyric Stage, Porkfilled Players), *TBA* (2g), and *The Sugar House at the Edge of the Wilderness* (Ma-Yi), among others. Carla is an alumna of the Women's Project Lab, the Lark Playwrights Workshop, the CTG Writers' Workshop, and the Ma-Yi Writers Lab. She is the former Artistic Director of the Asian-American theater company, 2g, and a proud member of New Dramatists. Carla has written for Amazon's *I Love Dick*, USA's *Graceland*, AMC's *Fear the Walking Dead*, and *The First*, forthcoming from Hulu. For more information: www.carlaching.com.

ANNAH FEINBERG's plays include *The Beautiful Beautiful Sea Next Door*, *Numismatics*, and *The Ivories*, and have been developed and produced by Ars Nova, Naked Angels, EBE Ensemble, The Blank, and Clubbed Thumb. She has served in artistic and literary capacities for the Civilians, LCT3, MTC, Steppenwolf, Northlight, ICM, TimeLine, and 13P. She wrote and directed the short film *Gretch and Tim*, cartoons @memyselvesand, and her musical web series *Balloon Room* is coming soon. She served as script coordinator on *I Love Dick*, and has assisted on *Arrested Development, Flaked, Damien,* and *Veep.* Annah has a MFA in dramaturgy from Columbia University. For more information: www.annahfeinberg.com.

SARAH GUBBINS's plays include *Fair Use, The Drinking Problem, The Kid Thing* (Jeff Award, Edgerton Foundation New American Play Award), *fml: how Carson McCullers saved my life,* and *Cocked.* Sarah is a Core Writer of the Playwrights' Center, a former Carl J. Djerassi Fellow and Jerome Fellow. She holds a MFA from Northwestern University. She lives in Los Angeles.

LAURA JACQMIN's plays include *Residence* (Actors Theatre of Louisville's 40th Humana Festival of New Plays), *January Joiner* (Long Wharf Theatre), *Ski Dubai* (Steppenwolf Theatre), *Dental Society Midwinter Meeting* (Chicago Dramatists/At Play, 16th Street Theater, Theater on the Lake, Williamstown Theatre Festival), *A Third* (Finborough), and *Look, We Are Breathing* (Rivendell Theatre). For TV, Laura has written for *Grace and Frankie* and *Lucky 7.* She worked on the videogames *Minecraft: Story Mode* and *The Walking Dead—A New Frontier: The Telltale Series.* Her awards include the Wasserstein Prize, two NEA Art Works grants, the Kennedy Center David Mark Cohen Award, and two MacDowell fellowships.

JOY MEADS is Literary Manager/Artistic Engagement Strategist at Center Theatre Group. At CTG, her dramaturgy credits include *Archduke* by Rajiv Joseph, *Good Grief* by Ngozi Anyanwu, *Appropriate* by Branden Jacobs-Jenkins, *Forever* by Dael Orlandersmith, *Marjorie Prime* by Jordan Harrison, *A Parallelogram* by Bruce Norris, *The Royale* by Marco Ramirez, and *Radiate* by Daniel Alexander Jones. Joy was Literary Manager at Steppenwolf Theatre Company and Associate Artistic Director at California Shakespeare Theater. Joy has developed plays with Oregon Shakespeare Festival, New York Theatre Workshop, Berkeley Rep, Denver Center for the Performing Arts, the O'Neill, Ojai Playwrights Conference, Portland Center Stage, South Coast Repertory, and Campo Santo, among others.

KELLY MILLER is a manager at The Shuman Company in L.A. She served as Director of Development for New Neighborhood, and as South Coast Repertory's Literary Director and Co-Director of the Pacific Playwrights Festival from 2009–15. She dramaturged more than forty world-premiere productions and readings at SCR, and created the CrossRoads commissioning project. Miller has worked at Actors Theatre of Louisville, Williamstown, Long Wharf Theatre, and consulted for the O'Neill, Berkeley Rep, the Kennedy Center, The Public Theater, Native Voices at the Autry, and many others. She has had residencies at Lake Tofte Center and SPACE on Ryder Farm. She serves on the board for the Women's Project Theater and is an Ambassador-at-Large for the National New Play Network. She develops new work with her company Creative Destruction.

MEG MIROSHNIK's plays include *The Fairytale Lives of Russian Girls* (Yale Rep, Alliance), *The Droll* (Undermain, Pacific Playwrights Festival), *The Tall Girls* (Alliance, O'Neill, La Jolla DNA Festival), and *Lady Tattoo* (Pacific Playwrights Festival, Rattlestick F*cking Good Plays Festival). Meg received the Whiting Award, an Alliance/Kendeda Graduate Playwriting Award, and was a Susan Smith Blackburn finalist. She has commissions from South Coast Rep, Steppenwolf, and Yale Rep. Meg is a Core Writer at the Playwrights' Center. She received her MFA from the Yale School of Drama.

DARIA POLATIN's plays include *Palmyra*, *In Tandem*, *Guidance*, *That First Fall*, *D.C.*, and *The Luxor Express*, inspired by her father's life growing up in Egypt. She has been produced at The Kennedy Center, Actors Theatre of Louisville, Naked Angels, Ensemble Studio Theatre, Golden Thread Productions, Noor Theatre, Malibu Playhouse, Cape Cod Theatre Project, and in London and Hong Kong. Daria is a member of the Center Theatre Group Writers' Workshop, the Echo Theater Writer's Lab, and has been in residence with London's Royal Court Theatre. She is an alumna of Youngblood. Daria has directed plays, and her short film *Till It Gets Weird*. She writes for the forthcoming series *Jack Ryan* (Amazon), and wrote for the psychic drama *Shut Eye* (Hulu). Daria's debut novel, *Devil in Ohio*, will be published by Macmillan. She received a Kennedy Center/ACTF Best One-Act Play Award, a Middle East America Playwriting Prize Honorable Mention, and was a Wasserstein Prize nominee and Princess Grace Award finalist. She has a MFA from Columbia University. For more information: www. dariapolatin.com.

TANYA SARACHO was born in Los Mochis, Sinaloa, México. She is a playwright who writes for TV (*How to Get Away with Murder*, HBO's *Looking* and *Girls*, and *Devious Maids*). She is the creator and showrunner for *Pour Vida*, (Starz, in development). She was named Best New Playwright by *Chicago Magazine*. Tanya's plays have been produced at Primary Stages, Second Stage, Denver Theatre Center, Oregon Shakespeare Festival, The Goodman Theater, Steppenwolf Theatre, Teatro Vista, Teatro Luna, Fountain Theatre, Clubbed Thumb, NEXT Theatre, and 16th Street Theater. Tanya was named one of nine national Latino "Luminarios" by *Café* magazine and given the first Revolucionario Award in Theater by the National Museum of Mexican Art. She is the founder of Teatro Luna (the first all-Latina theater company in the nation) and of ALTA (Alliance of Latino Theatre Artists). She is currently in development with Big Beach Films for a project about brujería, and has commissions from South Coast Repertory and Two Rivers Theater.

MARISA WEGRZYN is a Chicago playwright working in L.A. Her plays include *Mud Blue Sky*, *The Butcher of Baraboo*, *Hickory-dickory*, *Killing Women*, and *Ten Cent Night*, among others. She has been presented by Steppenwolf, Second Stage, Baltimore Center Stage, A Red Orchid Theatre, Chicago Dramatists, Theatre Seven, and Moxie Theatre, among others. Marisa is a winner of the Wendy Wasserstein Playwriting Prize. For TV, she has written for *Mind Games* (ABC), *The Mentalist* (CBS), and *Feed the Beast* (AMC).